PREFACE

ON May 17th, 1934, there came into force a new law relating to British birds, entitled *The Protection of Birds Act, 1933*. This Act makes it illegal to sell, offer for sale, or have in one's possession for sale, any live British bird to which the Act applies. In the Schedule to the Act appear the names of some 66 species, including all the Finches and Softbills commonly kept by British bird fanciers.

Just prior to this new Act being considered by a Standing Committee in the House of Commons, *Cage Birds* put before Lord Scone, now the Earl of Mansfield, (one of the members of the Committee) an amendment to the effect that closed-ringed aviary-or cage-bred specimens of the scheduled birds should be exempt from the Act. In due course this amendment, most ably sponsored by Lord Scone, was unanimously accepted by the Committee and embodied in the Act.

Thus it comes about that the only British birds fanciers can, henceforward, legally offer for sale are those bred in captivity and equipped with closed rings of correct size, which must be fitted when the nestlings are only a few days old.

In this book Mr. H. Norman, whose experience with British birds was lifelong, has gone very thoroughly into the general management and feeding of British Finches and Softbills.

E. R. W. LINCOLN
(Editor *Cage Birds*).

v

LIST OF ILLUSTRATIONS

BREEDING BRITISH BIRDS
IN AVIARIES AND CAGES

WINNING TEAM OF FINCHES
Bullfinch, Goldfinch, Siskin, Greenfinch and Linnet

BREEDING BRITISH BIRDS

IN AVIARIES AND CAGES

Housing, Feeding, Sexing and General Management
of British Hardbills and Softbills

By
H. NORMAN
Illustrations by R. A. Vowles

Revised   Edition

CONTENTS

Specialist Clubs for British Bird Breeders

All bird lovers interested in the breeding of our native species are strongly recommended to join the following clubs : —

The British Bird Breeders' Association

The National British Hardbill Society

The National British Softbill Society

Secretaries' names and addresses can be obtained from the Editor of *Cage Birds*

FOREWORD

By Hylton Blythe (Secretary, British Bird Breeders' Association)

AS a practical breeder of British birds for the past thirty-five years, and the first person to attempt to evolve a standard of leg-ring sizes for the various species, I was heartened by the amendment to the " Buckmaster Bill " (Protection of Birds Act, 1933), for I took this to be an indication that the *breeder* of British birds was at last recognised as a *bona fide* aviculturist and that his efforts were worthy of recognition and consideration. It seemed that a step forward had been taken from the stage where bird protection legislation was made regardless of the viewpoint of great numbers of people who made a close-up study, as it were, of the habits of the birds of their native land.

At the outbreak of the world war, British bird breeders were in possession of a range of ring sizes for various species which were reasonably satisfactory, and which were being improved upon as a result of research each nesting season. Fanciers all over the country co-operated in the task. Unfortunately, hostilities disrupted this process, and at the time of going to press with this new edition rings are restricted to three sizes instead of ten, as in 1939, owing to shortage of labour and material. However, with the development of new metal alloys and improved processes of manufacture, we can shortly look forward to a ring standard that will be entirely satisfactory.

Meanwhile, it is imperative that lovers of British

FOREWORD

birds should carry on breeding operations with a view to furthering knowledge and experience. Special attention should be given to the keeping of accurate breeding records. A few lines written in a book each day, or even each week, builds up an indisputable record, and after a few years one finds oneself with a veritable encyclopædia of reference.

Every bird bred in captivity should be recorded for the sake of future generations. *Cage Birds* and the local press will always find space for such records. A printed record sometimes results in a communication from another interested person in one's own district whose existence may have been unknown. This often results in a widened outlook by the interchange of experiences. So be sure to record nesting results in a strongly-bound book. And having made your own record, send items of special interest to *Cage Birds* and also to your local paper.

Another aspect of record-keeping which is neglected is the preservation of specimens of noteworthy birds which have died. Think what a priceless exhibition of rare-feathered British birds and Hybrids would now be available for the information of the younger generation if specimens had been systematically stuffed during the past fifty years instead of being consigned to the dustbin. All that is necessary is to skin and lightly stuff, with labels attached to the foot stating species, variety, sex and date. It is a simple process to have these " skins " prepared, and the taxidermist will give information regarding sex after dissection.

BREEDING BRITISH BIRDS

CHAPTER I

HOUSING AND FEEDING

EVER since the days of the ancient Chinese, Mexican and Egyptian civilisations wild birds have been caught and kept in cages and other enclosures as pets for their song as well as for their beauty of plumage, and this pleasure-giving practice has continued, with variations as regards housing and treatment, until the present time with very little restriction.

Now, however, seeing that it is illegal for professional catchers to trap birds for sale to dealers and individual fanciers we must build aviaries or provide ourselves with special cages with a view to inducing pairs of Finches and Softbills to nest and rear young under controlled conditions if we are to keep good numbers of our cheerful native songsters to enliven us and help us to forget for a while our everyday cares and worries.

And let this fact be borne carefully in mind: It is quite permissible as the law stands at present for a fancier to take, during the open season, a few wild birds for the pleasure of having them or breeding from them, provided they are not of a species protected throughout the year in every county in Great Britain, and provided also that no birdlime or live decoy birds are employed. But on no account must they be offered for sale. Progeny from them, if fitted at an early age with closed rings which cannot be removed as the birds develop can, of course, be offered for sale as genuine cage- or aviary-bred specimens.

Although the existing restrictions upon purchasing British birds tend to be irksome, the Wild Birds' Protection Act, 1933, will probably have the beneficial effect of bringing additional pleasure and interest to the activities of British bird fanciers, who from now onwards will do more than just feed and attend to the everyday wants of their stock of native birds.

Joy of Breeding Winners

There will certainly be an added joy in watching the pairing, nesting and rearing of young, and after a time the fancier's spirit of emulation to breed and exhibit something better than his fellows—a specimen more choice in shape or colouring—is bound to show itself. In the *breeding* of winners there should be much more cause for pride than in the mere buying of the best examples from among a batch of wildlings.

I feel sure that in a few years we shall see a great improvement in the British bird sections of our shows. The present-day varieties of Canaries are all descendants of the dowdy little green wild bird, and we have in Budgerigars a more recent example of what can be done by domestification and controlled breeding.

Already aviary-bred Budgerigars are much larger and finer birds than their wild Australian ancestors, to say nothing of the wonderful range of colours and perfection of markings that have been achieved. And all this has been accomplished in a few short years.

What has been done with Canaries and Budgerigars can be repeated with our lovely British birds. At first

Suggestion for a lean-to aviary with covered flight

they may not nest so freely, but each season will be one step onward, and the further we get away from the wild-caught bird the easier the task will become, until eventually they will breed as freely as Canaries.

The breeding of our native species in aviaries and cages is no new idea. It has been carried on in a quiet manner for many years. I have myself at times had an odd pair or two of Finches nesting more or less successfully, and, of course, hybrid breeders have used Finch hens for the production of the beautiful crosses we see on the show bench. Thus there is no question about fanciers' ability to breed them, given suitable conditions.

Every Encouragement Needed

The desire to reproduce their kind at certain seasons is present in all wild birds, and our job is to give them suitable housing and to encourage and assist them in every way possible to nest and rear young.

Various methods of providing suitable accommodation will come readily to mind. We can build outdoor or indoor aviaries, construct large, planted flights with a certain amount of shelter, or employ roomy breeding cages. Aviaries, which may be of all sizes and shapes, can be placed in almost any situation, though naturally, with wild specimens, a certain amount of seclusion is an advantage.

Many bird-keepers will, no doubt, favour a lean-to building because of its simplicity of design and erection. Most people have in their garden a boundary wall or fence, and even if one cannot utilise this as it stands for one side of, or as the back of the building, it offers something substantial to build against and thus means good, solid protection.

Now although an aviary can be of any size, it is desirable that it should be not less than eight or ten feet in length, since ample wing-exercise is most essential for breeding pairs. To prove how the birds enjoy a long enclosure, fix up two perches, one at either end and as far apart as possible. You will notice that all the birds use these perches in preference to any others. This is especially true at certain times of the day, such as the late afternoon; they will dart from one to the other as fast as they can fly.

Such exercise is, as already stated, good for them. It keeps them strong and healthy, and, therefore, fit to perform the duties you require of them.

Outdoor flight cage for use in a sheltered position

B

The height of the aviary should be five or six feet at the front with an extra foot added at the back to allow a good fall of rain water from the roof. And in order that the interior shall not get wet there thould be several inches of roof overlapping the walls of the building.

It is desirable that a certain portion of an aviary be boarded all round to serve as a shelter for the birds in bad weather, and as a hiding place when suddenly frightened. The inside can be left open or boarded up about half way. Some shelters are constructed with just a small door giving access to the flight, in which case a window should be fitted to light up the interior otherwise the birds will be reluctant to enter.

Protection Against Cats

Boarding up about eighteen inches of the wired front and sides will prevent trouble from cats, which have an unpleasant habit of sitting on the ground close against the wires, watching and alarming the birds. The woodwork will put a stop to this sort of thing.

When fitting the perches in a span-roof aviary, the highest one, if fixed up near the apex, should be as long as possible. Birds roosting for the night always prefer the highest perch, and, consequently, if this is too short there will be a good deal of quarrelling. Bickering, once started, is apt to continue, and as it is peace that one wants in a breeding aviary, one should be careful not to do anything that is likely to cause trouble.

Some may prefer an aviary with a large, open flight, and there is, of course, no real objection to this. It should be boarded round the bottom, and wire netting of not less than half-inch mesh used to cover it. All seed hoppers and feeding vessels should be placed under cover for protection against contamination.

In my opinion, an aviary should not be of open wire all round. I have never yet seen one so built that was a complete success, the owner having (generally at some trying period) to cover up part of it with sacking or tarpaulin material, which is seldom satisfactory and certainly not pleasing to the eye.

Although one might argue that birds at liberty are exposed to all the winds that blow, it must be borne in mind that they are able to move about and gain shelter from shrubs and trees, a thing they are usually quite unable to do when confined.

Preserving Woodwork

In newly-erected aviaries all woodwork should be treated before it is covered with wire. Some may like to use paint of a particular shade, but a preservative such as Solignum is much better, and can be obtained in many colours.

If a plain dark brown finish is not objected to, creosote looks well and preserves the wood, and, if put on hot, penetrates and dries quickly. A little Stockholm tar can be added to creosote with advantage; it gives more "body" and improves the preserving qualities.

The floor of an aviary is a matter that needs a good deal of consideration. If the whole structure is to be raised off the ground, a few joists across, with floor boards nailed to them, make an excellent, clean base that can be covered with sand or sawdust. The whole structure can be then raised a foot or so from the ground and supported by bricks at each corner.

If the aviary is a fixture, concrete makes the soundest

and cleanest floor, and one that can be scraped, brushed or be given a periodical scrub.

The concrete need not be of a great thickness. If the earth is well rammed down, an inch or so of concrete laid smoothly will be quite sufficient. Broken glass mixed with the earth prevents vermin burrowing underneath, while if ordinary earth mixed with glass is used for the floor it should be rammed down until quite smooth, and then covered with a good thick layer of sand and sawdust, or a mixture of sand and coconut fibre.

Concrete Floor Best

Wherever possible, however, I urge a concrete floor. It is sanitary, and the aviary may safely stand in the same position for years. With an earth floor, the soil must occasionally be renewed or the aviary moved to a fresh site when the floor becomes foul.

" Flights " or " flight cages " are actually small aviaries, or very large cages. These, like an aviary, can be of any size, but the usual dimensions are about four to six feet long and two feet from back to front. They can be placed outdoors in sheltered situations, raised a couple of feet or more from the ground; or they may be fixed up in a spare room in the house, or out in the garden in an open shed.

An ingenious development of this scheme is the " miniature aviary " invented and popularised by Mr. Percy Glover, of Fareham. Invaluable where space is limited, this arrangement gives the birds almost every advantage of the normal aviary.

Ordinary flight cages, exposed to the weather would quickly become ruined, but the little aviaries in

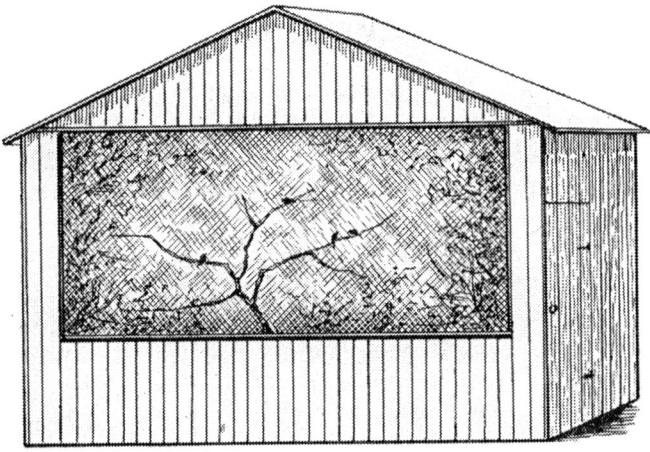

Straightforward style of aviary with apex roof and spacious wired front.
Boarding at the bottom protects the inmates from cats

question will withstand all conditions. Each section is intended for just one pair of birds.

A large open shed outdoors, equipped with a wire front, is probably the best and most successful method of housing prospective breeding Finches. They get plenty of light and air, and when accommodated in pairs are easily managed.

Although two pairs might be allowed in a large flight, a single pair will do better. The food supply for one species is not always the best for another, and obviously one should try to adopt the method that offers the greater chance of success.

Nearly all our British Finches have at various times been bred in ordinary breeding cages. These should not be less than about 30 inches in length with a sliding partition, either in the centre or, better still, making two compartments of unequal size. There are times when it may be advisable to part the pair for a short period.

In both flights and cages, the seed, food and water vessels should be so placed that they do not become fouled. It is desirable also to arrange them so that they can be easily refilled without undue disturbance to the birds.

Question of Furnishings

The manner of furnishing the aviary and flights for British bird breeding is a matter that requires careful attention. If we can make an enclosure resemble as far as possible a wild bird's natural surroundings we shall encourage and please the inmates, and advance one step nearer our goal.

It is a very good plan to buy some tile battens from a wood yard and nail lengths against the walls, about a foot apart, from top to bottom. Then fasten to this some fairly large mesh wire netting such as is used for poultry runs. Clumps of heather, furze and box trees can now be twisted into the wire in the corners and in other suitable places. Fix them in bunches, to make miniature trees or bushes in which the birds will probably build.

If the aviary is of fair size quite big bunches or faggots can be fastened and made secure with string or wire. This can be done both in the open flight and in the covered portion.

Should a pair select a bush in the open for nesting it is a simple matter to give them a little added protection by quietly laying a board on the wire immediately above the nest, putting a stone or weight on it so that it cannot be dislodged by the wind.

The following notes on aviaries suitable for pairs of Finches, and on sexing, have kindly been supplied by Mr. Victor Carr, who, along with his father, has been successful in breeding our native Finches and certain British Softbills over a period of years. He writes:

" With the exception of some half a dozen enclosures all our aviaries are single units situated about 10 yards apart, some being all wire and others half enclosed by wire and the other half boarded up, including the top.

" These half-covered aviaries are 6ft. high, 4ft. wide and 6ft. long, with two panes of glass at the bottom ends of the covered parts. They are eminently suitable for two pairs of birds and in normal times are quite inexpensive to construct.

" Another type of structure we use is the same as the above except that the width is only 3ft. It is surprising

Type of Finch breeding enclosure favoured by Mr. Carr

how that foot less makes such a difference in an aviary of this type; indeed, only *one* pair of British birds can really be expected to do any breeding in these smaller enclosures.

Canaries can be Added

" But if a pair of Canaries is included it is quite satisfactory. More than one pair of British birds are inclined to worry each other in a small aviary, especially when one goes near them, but Canaries are better behaved.

" One can almost compare this small outdoor accommodation to breeding birds in a cage, and in these diminutive aviaries I only place birds which have been used to a cage all their lives, and also very tame ones that do not show any sign of nerves or restlessness.

" Another type of aviary we use, measuring 6ft. × 6ft. × 6ft., is all wire, with a shelter shelf all round the top. This structure will easily accommodate three pairs.

" The shelf, I must explain, is of little use for nesting purposes as the birds much prefer to build their nests in small bushes tied high up on the wire, close to the underboard of the shelf. This board provides a good shelter for the top of the nest, and no damage can be done by thunder-storms.

" The shelf principle is an excellent one for shelter as the birds can get protection from strong winds, no matter from what quarter they blow. Furthermore, Canaries will readily build in a nest-box hung in the centre of the shelf.

" The final type of aviary we employ is 12ft. square, consisting entirely of wire, with the exception of the

four corners which are covered in to the extent of about
3ft. along both sides, the boarding extending 3ft. down.

" With a ledge made of wooden battens, or even wire
netting, right across these corners, one can put branches
of heather, evergreen oak, laurels, box, yew and other
evergreens thus providing four ideal nesting sites.

" With several more bushes spaced round the aviary
—made by fixing up a small bunch of heather, or any
of the above-mentioned evergreens in the centre—and
ramming one's fist in the top to make a place where
the birds can get started, one can expect five or six
pairs of birds to do well.

Points to Remember

" But there is one thing that must be impressed on
fanciers: Do not in any way restrict light from getting
into nesting sites, as the parent birds are then unable
to see the young birds' mouths when feeding. They
will nest in a dark spot as well as a light one, it is true,
*but they will not successfully rear their young in a
dark site.*

" Again, one must not expose nesting sites to any
violent rainstorms or the youngsters are likely to be
drowned or deserted. Protection round the sides of
the bushes one arranges in the open is a good thing,
but light must get in somewhere—either from the top
or, alternatively, from the sides.

" As regards a side-by-side range of enclosures, these
are known as control breeding aviaries and are quite
excellent for raising British birds, providing one
takes care in selecting the inmates of the various
compartments.

" For example, suppose you had a pair of Redpolls

in one compartment and you wanted to put up another pair. You must house this second pair as far away from the first as you are able, and in the intervening compartment put a pair of, say, Greenfinches.

The " Reducing " Process

" The reason for this is easily explained. Birds do not go to nest until they are in full breeding condition, and it is the male bird's duty to drive the hen to nest. By full breeding condition one means the elimination of superfluous fat, and no hen will nest if she is in too ' stout ' a condition.

" Thus the male bird chases his hen about until she has worked off all her superfluous fat and thereby gets her into hard breeding condition. If, then, you have two pairs of a species in compartments close together the most forward male bird would try to get into contact with the most forward female, and, as likely as not, such a bird would not be in reach of him. Therefore, he would be spending all his time and wasting all his energies on a bird that was not meant for him, and nothing would come of it.

" And now a few observations on the sexing of certain of our commoner British birds. The Goldfinch, Redpoll, Twite and Linnet are very difficult for the inexperienced to sex; indeed, the species I have mentioned can only be sexed with certainty in the hand.

" One cannot sex such birds with any accuracy when they are flying in an aviary, especially if the hen bird is a very good one, that is, from an exhibition point of view.

" The hen Goldfinch has small brown feathers on the butt of the wing, while the cock has black ones. If there seems to be little difference in this respect, have a look at the feathers on the nostrils, those which extend over the mandible. On a hen bird these are a buff colour, while in the case of a cock they are black.

Redpolls Tricky to Sex

" Redpolls are extremely difficult to sex and I do not think anyone can do the job with certainty when no

Design of aviary suitable for erecting at a corner of the garden. The double aspect has the merit of securing extra light and sunshine which the birds will enjoy

red coloration is to be seen. But as a last resort turn up the breast feathers with the fingers, when you will sometimes see just a slight pink colour on the very tips of a cock's feathers.

" Twites, if field-moulted, are easy to sex as the cock bird has a pink or red rump, never seen in the hen. When cage or aviary-moulted, this reddish colour disappears and then one can only sex them by the white bars on the flights. On a cock bird these are larger and also a purer white.

" This also applies to Linnets, but field-moulted cock Linnets have red on the breast, which, if not readily seen, can be observed by adopting the same procedure as mentioned in the case of the Redpoll.

" Most species of British Finches will agree, provided they have sufficient room to get away from one another.

In this connection fanciers have asked me if Hawfinches will agree with other birds in an aviary.

" One year we had a pair of Hawfinches with five or six other pairs of birds, and they nested and had young ones. Hawfinches are very confiding birds and become remarkably tame. The hen of this particular pair had to be lifted off her nest, and neither she nor the cock interfered with the other occupants of their enclosure, not even with a Chaffinch which was incubating within two feet of the Hawfinch's nest!

Breeding Companions

" Bramblefinches, renowned as noisy birds, especially at migrating seasons, are good companions in a breeding compartment and do not interfere with other birds, although they may snap at companions which come too close to them. But their ' bark ' is definitely worse than their bite.

" Buntings and Bullfinches are, perhaps, the most pugnacious of British Hardbills when breeding is in progress, and I advise would-be breeders of these species to keep an eye on them, especially the Buntings.

" On no account must these birds be put with another pair of their own species as they will fight to the death. Greenfinches also will quarrel a lot, but they can be bred on the colony system quite easily, especially if there are more hens than cocks. They quarrel among themselves but are not really vicious.

" Softbills are also like this. Robins, Nightingales and Redstarts in particular are pugnacious, especially when more than one cock of the same species is in close contact.

" I, personally, look upon this as Nature's method of

evening-up numbers. Hawks and other birds of prey are not very partial to these three species, and it seems to me that Dame Nature has so arranged it that these birds kill each other to a greater extent than in the case of other species.

Warning to The Lady !

" I have known a Robin scalp Hardbills in his thirst for blood, or, perhaps, just to show off his killing powers to his mate. Maybe, however, he desires his would-be mate to take note of what may happen to her if she does not abide by his wishes !

" So fanciers who may be attempting to breed these three kinds of Softbills must take particular care to introduce pairs tactfully and gradually.

" Take the case of the Redstart or Nightingale. All the winter, cocks and hens of both species fight each other, and not until they have their spring moult would I advise anyone to put them together.

" And even then I should arrange matters so that a cock bird is in one pen and a hen in an adjacent compartment so that they can see, but not be able to get at, one another. If this is done for about a week before putting them together they will have grown more or less accustomed to each other.

" When finally introduced, make sure they really do agree, and place in their quarters two food pots, as far away from each other as possible, so that there is no fear of one bird monopolising the food supply. This is very important.

" In conclusion, I ask fanciers to remember this : All birds, even Hardbills, are virtually Softbills in their feeding habits. The term " Hardbill " generally indicates a bird which nourishes its young by crop feeding, a Softbill being a bird which feeds its young solely from the mandibles, that is, by a process of placing live food, etc. straight into the youngsters' mouths.

" A seedeater (Finch, or Hardbill) eats its food and, when it is half digested, regurgitates it to the nestlings. But in the breeding season even Hardbills feed their babies in the same way as Softbills, and Bramblings, Chaffinches, Buntings and Hawfinches in particular really need a certain amount of live food, such as gentles (thoroughly scoured), live ants' cocoons, green-fly or any other handy grub."

Encouragement Necessary

Although spring is the normal nesting-time for all birds, in confinement they may need a little encouragement. Some will start building right away in a bush, or bunch of branches, as they would in a wild state, but the majority need something to begin with. We can hang ordinary Canary nest-pans in odd places, and we can do the same with nest-boxes.

These latter one can make of various sizes, four, five and even six inches in width and breath. A handful of moss or short hay can be put into them and worked round into the shape of a nest. The birds will pull some of this out and scatter it about, but that does not matter since it shows that they are interested, and later they will start collecting material with a definite object.

Another nesting receptacle is the pre-war type of German Roller Canary travelling cage with a few of the bars cut out, so that the bird can easily enter. Some twigs of heather should be twisted among the bars to give

One of Mr. Carr's aviary Bramblefinch hens which nested in a Roller
travelling cage with bars removed from one end

seclusion and a semblance of wild surroundings. Years
ago one could purchase wicker-work nests, but they have
now disappeared from the market.

Old wild birds' nests of any species are valuable;
they are taken to readily. If they are Thrushes' or
Blackbirds' nests and you need them for Finches, put
a handful of moss or hay in the bottom to give them a
start. Old Finch nests, however much they are broken,
can be used, and one can make them assume, more or
less, normal exterior shape with some rough material
and fix them in one of the bushes.

Birds such as Starlings should have a nest-box with
an entrance at the side, in fact, in a large aviary one or

two of these could be fixed up irrespective of the species
of bird kept.

I once had a hen Bullfinch that built in one and a
Greenfinch that built in a flower-pot. One never knows
just what our native birds will do when confined and
domesticated; part of their wild nature has gone, and
with it some of their natural habits.

When using cages for breeding, a short length of
wood should be fixed across one corner and a bunch of
heather or shrub be pushed into the angle. A nest-pan
thrust amongst these twigs will give the hen a start.

A Gratifying Spectacle

There are other arrangements that will suggest
themselves to keen bird breeders, and I do not know
of anything more interesting and pleasurable than to
see a hen Bullfinch taking to something that we have
arranged specially for her. To watch her building the
nest is particularly interesting, for her actions are quite
different from those of a Canary.

Although, later, I propose to deal with the feeding
of each species separately, a few general notes on the
subject here will not be out of place.

In normal times there is available a large assortment
of seeds supplied in a well-cleaned state by bird food
vendors. What with canary, hemp, rape, teazle, niger
and linseed, one would think nothing else was needed,
but of these valuable seeds only rape, linseed and teazle
are obtainable in the fields, and actually rape and its
near relatives charlock and wild mustard are the only
kinds at all plentiful.

In their natural state British Finches live on seeds
from wild plants that we call weeds, on the berries of

the hedgerows, and on insect life. Although the seeds we purchase will keep Finches in good condition and song, we need them to be in extra high fettle for breeding purposes, and few realise the difference between birds that are healthy and in song and those in really sound breeding condition.

Natural Foods Essential

I have many times seen a cock Linnet sitting comfortably on a swaying branch and singing his delightful song without any signs of emotion. Another, not far away, may be in genuinely high fettle, fairly dancing on his perch, his wings flapping, his throat swelling and his song pouring out in a most impassioned manner.

There is a difference. The second bird is in high breeding condition, the condition in which we want our aviary birds to be when they go to nest. To get them like this we must follow nature as closely as we are able. Those bird keepers who live in the country can collect bunches of useful material without much trouble, and suburban dwellers will find many plants growing on allotments and bare patches, and possibly a limited number in their own garden.

The real town man is somewhat handicapped, but he can get from the seedsman several valuable seeds, such as sesame, gold of pleasure, dandelion, thistle, cornflower, lettuce and one or two others, and with these he can make up a valuable mixture.

Well Cleaned Mixtures

Some firms put up an excellent wild seed mixture which they have obtained from farmers' threshings, and, after screening and re-screening to eliminate all

c

the dirt and dust, are able to offer it to bird keepers as an additional food for their pets.

Some of these mixtures are splendid for Finches, containing as they do many choice seeds that could be obtained in no other way. They can be purchased in packets and in 7lb. and 14lb. bags, and although not cheap the seed is well worth the price usually asked for it.

Another food that can be given with advantage is soaked seed. This can be used by everybody, but it is particularly valuable to those bird keepers who are unable to obtain half-ripe seeding wild food.

Dry seeds should be soaked for 36 hours in cold water, the water being frequently changed. It should then be strained off as dry as possible, and, if this is done overnight, and the strainer stood on one side and tilted a little, the seed will be in good condition for use in the morning. To keep up a constant supply two or three basins should be kept going.

If the seed is required in a hurry and there is not time to drain it thoroughly, a spoonful of dry biscuit meal or prepared food can be mixed with it to absorb the superfluous moisture. Sprouted seeds also provide valuable food.

Although it is possible to rear birds on seeds and bunches of seeding wild food gathered in the open, it is necessary to supply the parent birds with some kind of soft food, because our wild plants may fail us at a critical time, and there are some who cannot get them. If the Finches can be induced to take soft food it simplifies matters considerably.

Whatever soft food we decide to use, the birds should be got accustomed to it some time before they start nesting; it is folly to wait until the young have arrived before supplying it.

If the birds do not take to the food, a little should be mixed in a small supply of seeds fresh daily, but after a time it can be given separately.

The question arises as to what soft food should be given to assist the birds in the rearing of the young. Naturally, the first we consider is hard-boiled fowls' eggs, as being the nearest meaty food to insect life. All the yolk can be used with about one-third of the white, which should be mixed with powdered biscuits or brown breadcrumbs.

Brown Bread Preferred

The latter is to be preferred to white bread, and the birds seem to like it better. As a proof of this, if you place a small heap of each out in the open you will notice that the Chaffinches, Hedge Sparrows, Thrushes and Blackbirds prefer the brown, and even those greedy birds, the House Sparrows, will eat the brown first.

For those bird breeders who do not care to use hard-boiled egg, there are some good, ready-made foods upon the market. These are excellent and most useful if the birds are trained to eat them. But the food I like best, one that has been used successfully for the rearing of British birds, Mules and Hybrids, is a superior brand of insectile food as used for the feeding of British and Foreign Warblers.

The best of these foods will rear the most delicate youngsters. Fresh egg-food is, no doubt, of great value, and even when using insectile mixture as a stock food, a little can be given occasionally as a change. But one should be very careful with it, because when offered in any quantity regularly it does not seem quite to suit British Hardbills.

When Finches are once on soft food it is not difficult to get them to take a small portion of bread dipped in milk, and this, besides acting as a splendid corrective, affords excellent nourishment for the young.

CHAPTER II

THE GOLDFINCH

OF all our British seedeaters, the Goldfinch is undoubtedly the most popular. He is bright and cheerful, has an attractive song, and is gay in plumage, with some very effective splashes of bright colour about him.

His red face is quite different in appearance from that of any of the other Finches, and although some of them can boast an edging of pure yellow in the wings, none is quite so brilliant in appearance. He is well named " Goldiewing " and " Goldspark " by country people.

Most Popular Finch

We not only value the Goldfinch for his own sake as a songster and exhibition bird; he has also proved his usefulness as a producer of beautiful Mules both dark and light in plumage, and of wonderful Hybrids when crossed with other Finches. He is so valuable as a fancier's bird that we cannot do without him, and now to retain him we must definitely breed our own specimens, for the British Goldfinch is protected all the year round in all counties.

Fortunately, he is a bird that takes well to domesticated life; he is quite at home in aviary, flight, or cage, and has bred frequently in all such quarters.

The hens, if in good condition, will nest readily in

nest-boxes, pans, or wicker cages. They will build a beautiful nest, sometimes taking an old wild bird's home as a foundation. The nest is a compact, closely built structure, with a good strong felted rim, and to encourage a hen to make this we must supply her with the most suitable material, letting her take her choice and go about the building in her own way without any interference from her owner.

I have a nest in front of me composed of moss, fine roots, and dry grass stems, the outer structure being joined together with bits of lichen and spiders' webs. It is neatly lined inside with feathers, vegetable down and hair.

Where to Get Materials

Nearly all these materials we can supply without much difficulty. The fine roots we can find on the edge of a field or allotment, or we can pull up by the roots some coarse grass or herbage and lay it on the roof of the aviary to dry before putting it inside.

Moss we can gather or purchase in bunches at the nearest nurseryman's; dry grass stems should be broken into odd lengths; vegetable down we must hunt for, and we shall find it in waste places on old thistle stems, ragwort and goat's beard, also in neglected gardens on old plants that have not been cut down.

Cow-hair will not give us any trouble. We can easily get that either from the bird shops or in quantity from dealers who advertise aviary requisites. The nest-pans, boxes, and so on, should be fixed in position some time before they are required, to give the birds the opportunity to examine them and to make their selection.

The building material can wait until there are some signs of nesting by the birds, that is to say, when the cock or hen is observed playing with a bit of dry material. As soon as this is noticed a supply of the coarser kinds can be given, followed by others as the building progresses.

Typical British Goldfinch

When the hen has laid and begun to sit, she should not be interfered with; many a clutch of eggs has been spoilt by the bird's owner taking too great an interest in her maternal activities.

She will incubate about 13 days, and the behaviour of the pair will soon give one some clue as to what has happened. Supply soft food, a little soaked teazle and wild food and leave them as much as possible to themselves to get on with the job. As the young ones grow, increase the supply of the food of which the parents make most use.

Goldfinches are rather late in going to nest, and the very late ones frequently have only one nest; but with a good supply of proper food a second nest can be expected.

How to Sex Goldies

Some bird keepers experience difficulty in distinguishing the sexes of Goldfinches. Generally speaking they are very much alike, and there is not the distinction in colour that exists in some species. Cock birds have rather longer heads and are somewhat flat on the crown, with stoutish beaks.

If the bird is handled and the wing opened, the butt will be found jet black with a greenish flush when caught by the light. Turn him over on his back and one can see a decided yellow tinge on the breast. The red blaze of the face runs well back past the eye. The head of the hen is somewhat rounder with a rather less stout beak, and the butts of the wings have a brownish tinge to them.

The feeding of Goldfinches is a matter that requires careful attention as successful nesting depends so much upon the condition of the birds. Most fanciers have their own special seed mixtures, and although these vary in the proportions of the ingredients, the same seeds are nearly always included.

The following is a mixture that will keep most Finches in good condition:—Teazle seed 4 parts, canary 3 parts, hemp 2 parts, and linseed 1 part. Then to provide variety and assist condition one can give a little thistle, dandelion, maw, cornflower, and chopped walnuts; also a few sunflower seeds.

Our greatest aids to condition, and in keeping the birds in health during the nesting and rearing of the young, are the wild foods and seeding plants we can collect in the open. One of the first is dandelion, of which we can use both the leaves and ripening seed pods; and before this is finished we have sow-thistle, another plant that can be used in both ways. Then follow in quick succession chickweed, shepherd's purse, seeding grasses and a host of others.

Food Variety Desirable

A supply of these should be collected two or three times a week and given to the birds until the young arrive, and they should then be offered daily. It is by variety in food, and attention to their wants without fussing, that success is ensured.

When the young can feed themselves, soft food, soaked seeds and sprouted seeds should be supplied until they are well on to the usual seed mixture.

As already mentioned, the Goldfinch is a highly popular exhibition bird, and at most of the classic shows classes are remarkably well filled. Competition is very keen, winners from all parts of the country competing against each other at the " National " fixtures.

CHAPTER III

THE BULLFINCH

HERE we have another extremely popular cage bird, a bold, handsome, showy specimen very typical of his name. Although not much of a songster, his shape and beautiful colouring and his contented disposition, whether in cage or aviary, have always made him very much sought after as a drawing-room pet, aviary inmate, and exhibition bird.

Now that we are hoping to breed Bullfinches in quantity, in aviaries and cages, we shall, no doubt, in a few seasons note a great improvement in size, shape and colour, and as they will probably be free breeders when paired together (instead of to other species, which has hitherto been the usual lot of Bullfinch hens) we shall soon possess substantial aviary-bred stocks.

Young Hens More Reliable

Young hens are to be preferred as they are almost certain nesters, and take to the ordinary nest-pan or box without much trouble. Occasionally we may have one that does not, and then it becomes necessary to use any device that will encourage her. I feel sure that when these birds drop their eggs on the floor of the flight or cages, it is because they are not quite satisfied with their nesting arrangements.

The Bullfinch hen is a very prolific layer of eggs, and sometimes clutches follow too quickly. Where this is the case some of them can be transferred to Canaries or other foster parents. Although the hen has a rather bad reputation for sitting and rearing, we must not forget that her partner has usually been a cock of another species, and it is just possible that hens of this species

Perfection in a cock Bullfinch

will act better when paired up in a natural manner. I have known several pairs that have done well.

Bullfinches in a wild state pair for life and are very devoted and constant to each other. This being the case it is well to start with young birds, and, while healthy, keep the same pair together.

Although the hen in captivity will build with almost anything reasonably suitable that comes to hand, it is as well to supply her with the correct materials such as fine twigs, roots and hair, to which can be added a scrap of wool and a few feathers.

When nesting, the hen is shy and retiring, and whatever nest we use (either pan or box) it should be somewhat secluded. This can be managed by the arrangement of a few twigs of heather or shrub. Possibly a sheet of brown paper or cardboard can be tacked in the right position to give added privacy.

In a wild state the food of the Bullfinch consists of the buds of fruit and other trees, wild seeds and berries. A good seed mixture can be made up from two parts of canary and teazle, with a half part each of linseed, rape and charlock. A few sunflower seeds may be supplied daily. Hemp seed is not good for them and if used it should be given only very sparingly.

Additional Food Items

A spoonful of wild seed mixture will help to get them into condition, and then in the early spring we can offer budding twigs of fruit and hawthorn, dandelion, shepherd's-purse, sow-thistle, chickweed, and many others as they come into season. The fruit and berries of the garden can be offered during the summer months.

These items must be freely supplied when young birds are about, not forgetting the various seeding grasses which are so valuable when old birds are rearing, and which will often induce them to feed when they are slacking off.

The novice should have no difficulty whatever in sexing these birds, as only the cock has the red breast.

CHAPTER IV

THE LINNET

IT is doubtful if any other of our native birds has achieved a popularity equal to that of the Linnet as a singing pet. He is not a particularly attractive bird as far as appearance goes, but as a songster he is the sweetest of all our Finches. When in condition he will sing the whole of a long summer's day.

So popular is he for singing contests and exhibitions that we cannot afford to lose him as a cage and aviary bird. Although of a rather nervous disposition he takes kindly to domestication and quickly settles down to enjoy his life with the good things around him.

A Free-breeding Species

Linnets are free breeders and will produce two or three nests during the season. A pair properly mated become devoted to each other and should not be parted while they remain in health.

In an aviary or large flight open to the air, the hen will take to a nest-box, or rough foundation for a nest placed in a clump of gorse and heather, and will build a most charming nest equal to that of any Finch. When filled with the clutch of reddish spotted eggs it makes a delightful picture.

The cock can be safely trusted with the eggs and is attentive to the sitting hen. Although she is a close sitter and not easily disturbed, it is as well to pretend not to see her when attending to her daily wants, for however tame she is one cannot treat a wild-bred Finch quite as we do the domesticated Canary.

For building the nest, we must supply a few very fine birch twigs, grass stalks, moss, a few small feathers, hair, vegetable down, and a little wool. I have seen the cock assisting the hen in the construction of the nest and between them they make a cosy home.

I do not think there are any other Finches which feed so generally upon seeds as does the Linnet. When at liberty, rape, charlock and wild mustard form the principal food, although many other plants are included as they come into season and ripen.

Sound Staple Mixture

When caged we must not overdo the rape and charlock, as these seeds, if given alone, cause the birds to become rather loose in the bowels. A mixture should be made up as follows:—3 parts of canary, 2 parts of teazle, and 1 part each of rape, charlock and linseed.

This makes a splendid staple mixture, and we can provide variety by offering a little genuine wild seed mixture, and occasionally a little gold of pleasure, niger, plantain, sesame and thistle, also a few grains of sound hemp.

Linnets are rather difficult birds to get on to soft food; some, indeed, will not look at it, so that feeding them when they have young ones is not an easy matter. To get over this difficulty we must rely mostly upon soaked seeds, some of them just soaked and strained off, others allowed to sprout.

If possible, bunches of wild food should be gathered. The favourites are chickweed and shepherd's purse, the

latter collected very carefully so as not to scatter the
ripe seeds near the root of the plant. Groundsel, seeding grass, wild mustard and many others can be
included.

Linnet with superior markings

To most people the sexes in Linnets are alike in
general appearance, but to the eye of a fancier there is
a fairly pronounced difference. Cocks are generally
bolder and fuller about the head, richer in colour,
especially upon the back.

The breast and body markings are rather different,
and if the bird is caught, laid on its back, and the

breast feathers turned up with a pencil, the cocks will show a reddish moon near the edge of each feather. The hen does not have this dark mooning but each feather shows a distinct stripe down the centre.

Some fanciers will tell you that the cocks have whiter primary feathers in the wings, but I do not think this is altogether reliable. I have seen some hens with a greater display of white than many cocks.

Linnets for exhibition purposes should possess rich brown plumage on the back and a distinct pattern of mottling upon the breast. They must be shapely specimens and stand up fairly straight from the perch. A Linnet which crouches or " hugs " the perch seldom adopts a better pose even when perfectly tame.

Red Tinge Disappears

The breast markings undergo appreciable change, as a rule, under controlled conditions, and it is very rare that a breeder is able to bring about the delightfully ruddy tinge which is such a pleasing characteristic of a wild Linnet when it assumes full breeding plumage in the spring.

The markings on the throat must be distinct, and the colour surrounding them of a rich yellowish hue. A really good exhibition Linnet will always be seen to have some beautiful gyrations on the top of the head, in fact, a bird cannot be regarded as first-rate without them. Wings should be braced tightly to the body, with distinct white bars and a decided spangling at the tip of the feathers.

CHAPTER V

THE GREENFINCH

I FIRMLY believe that the bold Greenfinch is the commonest bird we have in the open fields and hedgerows. Proof of this lies in a day's birds'-nesting in open country where there are hedges and small plantations, for although one may find nests of many species, perhaps a colony of Linnets or several Chaffinches, none of them will compare with the number of Greenfinches that can be located.

These birds nest early and late. We can find them in the spring when there is scarcely sufficient foliage to hide the nest, and we can see them in late autumn, even after the harvest has been gathered and the fields are bare; and each brood of four or five youngsters is generally safely reared.

No Songster but Popular

Although the Greenfinch is not notable for his song, he has been a popular cage bird for many generations. It has usually been a brood of " Green Linnets " with which the country schoolboy has made his first attempts at hand-rearing, and no lustier or stronger birds could be selected for the purpose.

It will be no hardship for the fancier and bird lover to breed Greenfinches, as these birds nest readily in aviaries, flights and cages. After a few years' breeding one can imagine the great improvement brought about

D   37

by breeders—superior size, colour and shape. Besides, there is always the possibility of a break in the plumage under domestication. This would soon enable us to breed variegated, marked and clear specimens.

No wild bird to my knowledge will breed quite so freely in an aviary or flight as a pair of tame Green-finches. If well fed and looked after they will be the first to nest in the spring, and continue to do so right through the summer until the autumn moult.

One pair which I kept did so well that I had as many young Greenies as I could manage, so I turned them out in the late summer months. I thought they had finished, but no. They built one more nest in the branches of a climbing plant almost touching the roof of the aviary, and still demanded their share of the soft food when the enclosed youngsters were being fed.

Not Fussy about Nests

Old wicker cages, or an old wild bird's nest tucked away in a bush, will be preferred by the hens as nesting sites, although they will build in anything. Alternatively, the " foundation " can be fixed up in a bundle of furze or broom.

When breeding with Greenfinches in a cage, give them a nest box in preference to a pan and let it be of good size, say, about six inches square, so that there is room in it for a good wad of rough nesting material.

Hang the box fairly high up, quite half-way, and put it at the most secluded end of the cage, if necessary masking the top part of the cage with paper or cardboard. These precautions are not absolutely necessary in all cases, but they help towards success and, anyway, are not much trouble.

Shapely male Greenfinch

When building their nests in the open, Greenfinches are not so particular about the material they use as are most other Finches. It is not often that we can find two nests quite alike, and if we do it is because some particular substance is very common in the district.

As an instance, I once found two nests not far from each other, both of which were composed almost entirely of hay—quite an unusual occurrence, as hay is generally used with other material.

In most cases Greenfinches will build a rather large

nest for their size, composed of twigs, coarse roots, dry grass, and a little moss. The interior is of good shape and finished off quite neatly (for such a clumsy bird) with finer roots, a little wool, hair and feathers.

If our aviary specimens are supplied with moss, short lengths of grass with the roots attached, hair, cotton wool and a few feathers, they will put together quite a good nest.

A Hearty Feeder

The Greenfinch is a rather gross feeder and probably one of the easiest birds to cater for, but like all others he responds to good treatment. In a wild state he is mostly a good eater with a taste for newly-sown wheat and oats and liking a good share of the harvest in the autumn; but at other times he clears the land of charlock, dock, wild mustard, and many kinds of grass seeds. As a staple food we can offer him canary, rape and teazle. The best mixture is as much canary seed as the other two put together.

Occasionally he can have a little linseed, hemp and sunflower seed, especially if he should be located in an aviary where the extra exercise will counteract the fattening properties of these seeds.

A pinch of good wild seed mixture makes a change. Then there are the berries of the hedgerow, seeding grasses and other wild plants, all of which will be picked over and help to keep him healthy and fit.

When nesting, all these materials can be given, as well as some kind of soft food. As regards the latter he will not give us much trouble, taking almost anything offered to him. But such food should be of fairly good quality and not just rough chicken meal.

I know some pairs have reared young on chicken meal, but although they were fairly lusty youngsters they would probably have been better had they been brought up on more digestible food.

Soaked and sprouting hemp and sunflower seeds are good, and half-ripe ears of corn will be eagerly taken. A fancier could grow some of this in the corner of his own garden if Sparrows and other wild birds were not too plentiful.

Young Greenies being heavy feeders the parents should be well supplied with food, particularly in the early morning and about four o'clock in the afternoon, when they start feeding in earnest after a mid-day slackening off.

Cocks Bigger and Brighter

The bird keeper should have no trouble in distinguishing the sexes of Greenfinches, since, as a rule, the hen is not so large as the cock and is much duller in plumage. The yellow in the wing of the cock is more pronounced than in the hen, her outer primary feathers being only edged with yellow.

There is more yellowish coloration in the plumage of the male bird, the hen's feathering being mostly a dull, greenish brown. Young Greenfinches resemble their mother in general plumage, but the cocks are usually the larger, with a bolder appearance especially about the head and beak, and brighter colour in the wing bars.

After the moult, of course, they take on their adult plumage, which simplifies the matter of sexing them because we have others from the same brood, and, comparing one with the other, we can decide which are the cocks.

This is a matter of some importance because we may get young cocks in one brood very little brighter in colour than some of the hens in another; but in the same brood the distinction is usually more apparent.

A class for male Greenfinches is provided at all open shows which schedule a British bird section, and very popular this class is, too. Some of the most outstanding specimens have been aviary-bred from parents of superlative merit.

Points in a Show Specimen

Requirements in an exhibition Greenfinch are extra good size and richness of colour. He must also be well-proportioned; that is to say, the large body must be accompanied by a large, bold head. These Finches vary a great deal in this respect. Other show points are broad shoulders, well filled in, good wing carriage, and a full breast with a nice curve from chin to vent.

Some exhibitors colour-feed their show-birds, but this is a practice that is to be deplored. The plumage of a good specimen is most attractive in its natural state.

Unfortunately, many colour-fed Greenfinches staged by experts have excellent size and shape. They are also put down in the best possible condition. They would have headed their class in natural plumage, but less experienced exhibitors often imagine that the colour-feeding has weighed with the judges.

CHAPTER VI

THE CHAFFINCH

ALTHOUGH the Chaffinch has not been of much use to breeders for the production of Mules and Hybrids—only very few genuine Hybrids from this cross having been recorded—these rarities have, as may be imagined, proved particularly interesting.

The crosses evolved have been Chaffinch-Bramble-finch, Chaffinch-Greenfinch and Chaffinch-Siskin, though in my life experience of cage bird shows I have only seen a single specimen of the last-named cross, though others may, possibly, have been produced. Anyway we hope to see more, and to get them we must do our best to retain the Chaffinch parent.

A Delightful Pet

As a cage bird and songster he is one of the gayest. His plumage is conspicuously bright, and when in breeding condition with his blue cap and ruddy breast he is particularly attractive and intelligent, has a lively manner and usually greets his attendant with a cheerful note.

One cannot consider the Chaffinch to be a high-class songster, and yet, years ago, they used to figure at singing contests. Now they are out of favour, the great increase in the Roller Canary singing contests having probably turned their sport-loving owners' attention in another direction.

Still, Master Chaffie is very popular as an exhibition bird and a few of them are nearly always to be seen at even the smallest shows.

It is not only the cock that is prized as a show bird. Hen Chaffies, of recent years, have come very much into favour. These attractive little ladies make quite successful exhibits in a mixed class for hens, with their sleek plumage and bright manner.

That being so, we have a double purpose in view when breeding this species, for we may turn out winners of both sexes, and, of course, all are useful for breeding purposes the following year.

Hens Most Responsive

Chaffinches have been reared both in aviaries and cages. The cock is an ardent and attentive partner, while the hen is most adaptable. If well treated, she gets quite " chummy " with her owner, and is always on the look-out for a special tit-bit, mealworm or spider.

The breeder who will go to some pains to get his hens, of whatever species, on friendly terms with him, stands a much greater chance of success than one who does not take this trouble. Most hens undoubtedly respond to good treatment, and it is an added pleasure to see how trustful they become.

When at liberty the Chaffinch builds the most compact and charming nest of all the Finches. It is of the felted type, strong and well put together. I have located scores of nests of this variety in my time, and been struck by the diversity of the materials used in building them. Whatever they are made of they are always skilfully finished.

If one has a choice I would advise that a pair of these

birds be provided with a large flight cage to themselves in an outside building as the cock is inclined to be pugnacious in the breeding season.

In a big aviary where the pairs have lived amicably together during the winter they should do well; but it is when birds in high condition are thrown suddenly together that trouble usually occurs.

An old wicker cage or nest-box fixed up and partly

Good example of a Chaffinch

hidden with foliage would be most likely to start them building. The materials for the purpose should be moss of various kinds in plenty, dry grass, fine roots, a little wool, a scrap or two of paper, feathers, hair and vegetable down.

The hen is the builder while the cock fusses around. They take several days to complete the nest, adding a bit now and again, until one wonders if they mean business or not. As a new nest is made for each brood it is as well to fix up more than one cage or nest-box before the season actually starts. The hen is a close sitter and not easily disturbed.

Sprouting Seeds Favoured

The food of the Chaffinch is mostly seeds and small insects. He is rather a dainty feeder and appears to prefer the seeds softened and sprouted. In the spring he makes himself rather a nuisance to the gardener when his seeds have just begun to swell.

This fondness for sprouting seeds we must not forget, and by keeping rape, turnip and radish seeds moist and warm for a few days we have an ideal food for this species and one that is particularly useful when young are being fed.

If sown thickly and allowed to get well started it can be cut out in squares and both the roots and growth given to the birds. As a stock food I like the following mixture:—Canary and teazle, 4 parts of each; rape, charlock and linseed, 1 part of each. A few sunflower seeds can be given daily and a small feed of hemp once a week.

Mealworms and other live food must be available, especially in the spring and summer months. They will eat live ants' cocoons, smooth caterpillars, grubs, earwigs, spiders, greenfly, gentles, wasp grubs, etc.

During the winter the old birds can have an occasional feed of mashed walnuts, which take the place of the beech nuts they would get if at liberty.

Chaffinches are not particularly keen on green food, but all the well-known plants should be offered, such as chickweed, shepherd's purse, groundsel, dandelion and so on. These should be gathered very carefully and given in bunches; the birds will look them over keenly and find many tiny insects among them.

Insectile Food and Suet

The best soft food is a good brand of insectile mixture made moist, although I have had them eat it dry. A small portion of finely-chopped suet can sometimes be added to it when insects are scarce. The soft food should be offered to them some time before they go to nest so that they will take it freely when needed.

Even a beginner should have no trouble in distinguishing the sexes, the cock alone having the ruddy coloured breast and the bluish cap. The hen is quite soberly clad but shows the Chaffinch wing with the white shoulder patch. She is shy and retiring in her manner compared with the cock.

CHAPTER VII

THE BRAMBLEFINCH

A S a cage bird, the Bramblefinch is not quite such a favourite as the Chaffinch, possibly because he is not a British breeding species, and not quite so trustworthy with other birds.

Our specimens are obtained from the flocks that visit us during the winter months and leave early in the spring for their breeding quarters in Northern Europe. We are told that their nest is somewhat similar to that of the Chaffinch but a shade larger and not quite so neatly finished.

Handsomely Garbed Birds

When in full colour these birds are very handsome and can generally hold their own against other Finches on the show bench. At fairly important shows they either have a class to themselves or compete against Chaffinches.

There are, no doubt, many bird lovers who would like to put up a pair for breeding, and I would advise them to house the two birds in a fair-sized flight cage, giving them a nest-box or other receptacle pushed into a bunch of birch twigs. Green moss, fine grass, a few feathers, vegetable down and broken-up pieces of birch bark should be supplied.

The general treatment and feeding should be the same as for the Chaffinch, a bird which they closely resemble in many ways. The sexes are not difficult to distinguish, the cock being much brighter in plumage with an orange tawny breast; the hen is appreciably duller and browner in colour.

Bramblefinches for the show bench must be staged in the best possible condition if they are to meet with

Grand specimen of a Bramblefinch

success. A large specimen always appeals to a judge provided it is shapely also. Some Bramblings have a ring of light feathers round the eyes. This gives them a rather queer appearance, as if they are suffering from sore eyes. They are useless for show purposes.

CHAPTER VIII

THE SISKIN

THIS delightful little bird breeds much more extensively in Northern Europe than it does with us. It nests annually in Scotland and parts of Ireland, but our cage specimens have been mostly obtained from the large flocks visiting us during the winter.

The sprightly Siskin is very popular as a cage bird, not only for exhibition, but also for breeding Mules with the Canary, and choice Hybrids with other Finches.

Most Friendly Disposition

No other Finch becomes quite so tame and friendly as the Siskin. The bird lover can quickly get one to take a grain of hemp seed from the fingers or come on to the hand for a choice morsel, and when once steadied this attractive bird is equally at home in either cage or aviary.

That being so, there is no need to put wild specimens in an aviary when, with a short period of cage life and a little extra attention, they can be made so tame.

In this bird we have a species that can be greatly improved by careful selective breeding; we can get them larger, with a more expansive bib and cap, and more even and richer in colour. The pencilling, a point in which many birds fail, we can improve and make much more sharply defined on both flanks.

Siskins take so readily to aviary and cage life that a pair will be quite happy and contented. I have had them escape from a garden enclosure for a day or so, but they soon returned and wanted to get in again.

In an aviary or large flight they will build a cosy nest, lay five or six eggs, and do their best to rear the young ones. For nesting purpose give them a couple of German Canary travelling cages (if you can get hold of any) with two or three of the bars removed from one end. Surround these with a fir branch and the result is an almost natural site for them.

Need Plenty of Exercise

These birds have been bred in cages but do better in an aviary or large flight. In the latter the cock can be trusted with more confidence, and the extra exercise taken helps to keep them fit. They are otherwise very liable to put on fat and become heavy and lazy, thus getting out of condition for a second nest.

Siskins should be fed carefully. A plain diet of canary, rape and teazle is best for them, with a little wild seed mixture for a change. A few grains of hemp can be offered when getting them into breeding condition and when feeding the young, but otherwise this seed is too fattening. All the usual wild plants can be freely given, not forgetting seeding grass which is so useful when they are rearing young.

As a rule one has no trouble in getting these birds to take soft food. A good insectile mixture is preferable to hard-boiled egg and biscuit. They will eat the latter freely but it is not good for them.

Siskins will take mealworms, small caterpillars, green-fly and various other live food, and such food should be supplied, if possible, during the nesting period. Soaked seeds are also useful.

For nest-building purposes Siskins should have fine roots, birch twigs, grass stalks, moss, vegetable down and hair.

The hen Siskin is easily distinguished from the cock. She has not so much colour generally, is very much streaked and marked, and has no black cap like the cock. It is best to remove the young ones as soon as they can feed themselves, and gradually get them on to the usual seed mixture.

The perky little Siskin

CHAPTER IX

THE REDPOLL

R EDPOLLS are probably the most adaptable of all
our Finches for breeding in aviaries, flights and
cages. They have bred freely under controlled conditions, and had it not been so easy in years gone by to
procure them from dealers they would, no doubt, have
been more widely cultivated.

Although I have not seen a specimen of the cross, I
believe the Lesser and the Mealy (or Greater) Redpoll
have been paired, but I think myself that the two species
should be kept quite distinct. They each have
characteristics of their own that might be developed,
and in each case more perfect show birds might well
be evolved.

Nesting Habits

The Lesser Redpoll breeds mostly in Scotland and
the North, but I am inclined to think that many nests
are overlooked in the Southern Counties. I have found
several myself on the wooded hills in Kent.

It is a deep, beautifully rounded structure, somewhat
smaller than that of the Linnet (for which it has
probably been often mistaken) built of moss, fine
twigs, roots and grass stalks, and smoothly lined with
feathers, vegetable down, and hair.

Although the Redpoll usually has just the one nest
in a season when at liberty, aviary-bred, well-fed birds
are more prolific.

E   53

It is no trouble to get Redpoll hens to nest. They will build in a nest-box, small wicker travelling cage, or coconut husk. Several of these receptacles should be hung about in various positions, and the birds allowed to make their choice.

Supply them with the building materials that they use in a wild state, and leave them as much as possible to themselves. If they are in an aviary or large flight they can usually be trusted to incubate the eggs and rear the young.

A stock seed mixture suitable for them is the same as that supplied to the Linnet, that is, canary 3 parts, teazle 2 parts, rape, charlock and linseed 1 part of each.

Lesser Redpoll in a characteristic pose

Cobby type of Mealy Redpoll

A little hemp can be given in cold weather or when getting them into breeding condition, but it should be supplied in quite small quantities and lightly cracked, as it is rather a heavy task for a Redpoll with his small beak to break open such large seeds. Offer a wild seed mixture and the various seeding wild foods one can collect.

When young are being reared a soft food of some kind should be supplied to the parents. I know of some Redpolls which were successfully reared just before the war on a well-known brand of packet seed, but it is as well to supply them with soft food occasionally while they are building and incubating.

The sexing of Redpolls is not an easy matter, unless the birds are field-moulted. In that case the cock has a rosy breast and a richer colour on the rump. In house-moulted birds one can only trust to the song of the cock, who has, perhaps, a shade more colour and blacker pencilling than the hen.

Show Points to Study

In choosing a cock Lesser Redpoll for exhibition one should pay special regard to size, colour and markings. The wing-bar should be clearly defined and sweep perfectly across the wing. Striping requires to be plentiful, and if the bird carries a good bib that will count in its favour.

At most shows Redpolls have to compete with Twites and Siskins, the result being that they sometimes have to take a back seat, as it were. However, if a judge is a first-rate British bird expert he sees that any Redpolls in a mixed class get full consideration.

The Mealy Redpoll can be exhibited at any show where a class is provided for Redpolls, that is, if the Lesser is not specifically mentioned. The chubby type of Mealy is the one most favoured by the majority of judges. Essential show features in a Mealy are size, pleasing shape and distinctness of lacing. The interior of show cases for Redpolls should be of a dark holly colour.

CHAPTER X

THE TWITE

THE Twite has never been quite so popular with southern fanciers as it deserves. It is true that it does not compare favourably with the Linnet as a songster, but it is a much prettier bird, having more colour and a greater variation in plumage.

Twites are northern birds, breeding in Scotland and the north of England. They come south in flocks during the winter months, mixing with the Linnets and others on the marshes and open fields.

Provide Insect Food

In an aviary or large flight they will nest and rear their young if properly fed. In this connection it must be borne in mind that although they are seed-eaters they feed the young mostly on insects during the early stages.

When they are due to hatch it is as well to supply them with a fair amount of greenfly or any other live food that can be collected. Bunches of grasses will often contain live insects among the seeding tops, and a little soft food of good quality should not be forgotten.

The young are rather slow to mature and there should be no slackening of the proper food when they leave the nest. The cock should look after them while the hen prepares another home for a second clutch of eggs.

The Twite or " Mountain Linnet "

Keep them well supplied with nesting material, which should consist of fine roots, twigs of heather, wool, feathers, and vegetable down. The sexes are easily distinguished, the cock having a reddish rump, which is absent in the hen.

As in the case of most seed-eating British birds, size

counts a great deal when it comes to selecting a Twite for competition at the shows. And in addition to size your potential exhibition specimen should be rich in colour and heavily marked all over, the breast markings being larger and more clearly discernible than those of a Linnet.

The head requires to be nice and full, also the neck. There must be no suspicion of meanness about the bird's top-end. Chubbiness in build, with perfect wings and claws, are other essential features.

A Desirable Feature

In an almost perfect specimen the white in the wings will be found to show up distinctly. This is a point that is only rarely seen, in fact, most otherwise excellent Twites fail lamentably in this respect.

To be successful in keen competition a cock of this species must be staged in absolutely perfect feather; it must also be well trained and quite steady when its cage is handled by a judge.

Twites like Siskins are very ready to put on fat under controlled conditions of life, and undue plumpness definitely spoils the graceful contour of a bird.

A moderate quantity of small insects and an occasional mealworm during the spring and summer months will go a long way to keep a Twite in the best of health and plumage.

CHAPTER XI

THE HAWFINCH

MANY bird lovers will no doubt try to breed from a pair of our largest Finches, and there is no reason why they should not succeed.

Hawfinches have nested in aviaries on several occasions. In a wild state they are shy, retiring birds, particularly during the breeding season, and, therefore, some special precautions are necessary when getting them to nest in enclosures. We must give them ample space, together with a certain amount of privacy.

They usually nest in a well-sheltered position in an orchard or among the dense branches of a fir, yew or holly, the nest resembling that of a Bullfinch, though somewhat larger. It is made of twigs, roots and grass stalks, and is lined with dry grass, fine roots and hair.

Outdoor Aviary Required

For breeding purposes a small aviary should be given up entirely to a pair of these birds, and a thick branch of fir, box or other evergreen should be fixed in one corner, with an old nest of any large species pushed into it.

For building, supply birch twigs, roots and the dry stalks of the wild plants given to the other Finches, dry grass and hair. Do not disturb the birds more than is absolutely necessary, particularly the sitting hen. Just give them food and water and leave them to themselves.

Mr. J. S. Hepburn, of Jersey, was very successful in

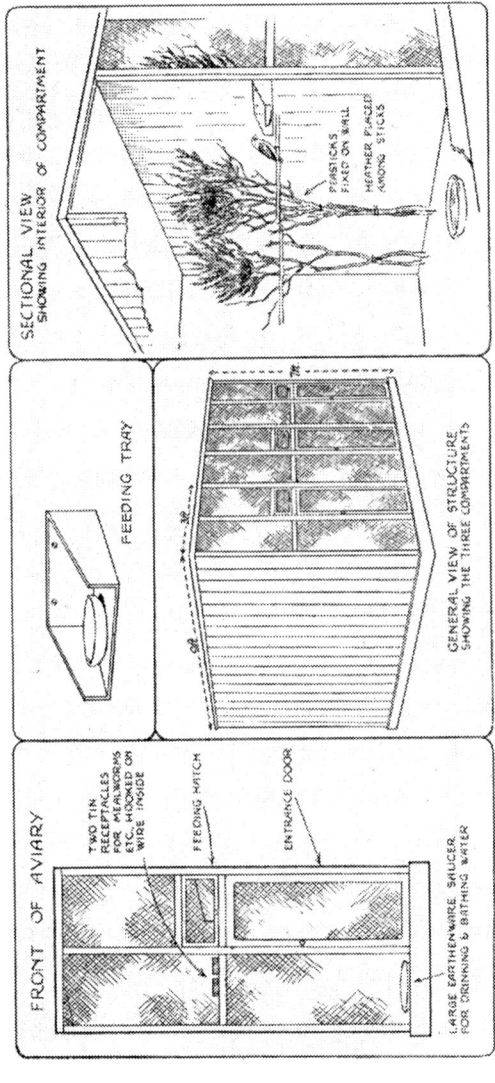

From the above illustrations a clear idea will be gained of the type of enclosure used by Mr. H. S. Hepburn (Jersey) for housing three breeding pairs of Hawfinches breeding these handsome birds during the year just preceding the war. His pairs were accommodated in separate compartments outdoors, a special feature of their design being the considerable depth of 9ft. which gave the occupants a feeling of security.

Some half a dozen young birds were reared to maturity, the principal rearing materials being meal-worms and other live food. This fancier maintains that he could have raised many more youngsters had live food been available in greater quantity. This is what he has to say concerning his housing and feeding methods with these birds:

Paired up in April

" During the winter months my pairs flew together with other Finches in a large outdoor aviary, and about the middle of April they were caught up and placed in an enclosure the front of which was all of wire netting with a concrete floor.

" This structure was divided into three compart-ments, each one being approximately 3ft. wide, 7ft. high and 9ft. deep. This considerable depth I found most important as it gave the birds a sense of security which they obviously appreciated.

" One pair of these handsome birds was installed in each compartment, suitably screened from viewing the birds in the adjoining compartment.

" The aviaries were furnished with a few stout perches, bunches of heather (the variety that grows here in Jersey in thick bushes about 2½ft. high) being placed in and around peasticks. Branches, etc., were fixed on the walls, and one or two old Blackbirds' nests and wicker baskets arranged in likely nesting sites.

" I supplied a variety of building materials but found the birds were content to line a chosen nest with dried grasses and lengths of sisal cord teased out.

" In my early experiences with these Hawfinches I discovered that to rely on them building thir own nests was fatal, in fact, I lost quite a few eggs owing to their futile efforts at home-making.

" From now on I gave the pairs mealworms every day, and any other live food to be found in the garden. This, together with sunflower seed, fruit tree prunings, seeding weeds, etc. soon brought them into condition.

" About this time the cocks were to be seen following the hens about, usually with a twig or strand of nesting material in their beaks. They displayed in that curious manner peculiar to the Hawfinch.

Little Material Used

" Occasionally both cock and hen would visit the nest and place a few strands of material in it. Although the hens seemed to make a lot of fuss over building operations, very little material was used up.

" The first eggs appeared about the second week in May, four or five being the average clutch. The hens sat closely, their mates occasionally offering them some tit-bit or other while incubation was in progress.

" On the morning of hatching, a fortnight later, I exercised more caution in approaching the compartments. I fed the birds as quickly as possible, avoiding direct glances at the sitting hens.

" The usual signs of hatching were eggshells on the floor and the parents uttering a peculiar clucking sound. I gave them mealworms and continued to offer

The dignified Hawfinch

this food at two-hour intervals, my wife taking over while I was at work!

" When home for lunch I was able to pop into the enclosures any live food available in the garden. The supply of mealworms was supplemented each day with a few small, striped, soft-shelled snails which the old birds seemed to relish greatly.

" Cherries, apple cores, fresh green peas, soaked sunflower and seeding weeds were provided, but I cannot recall seeing the parents passing on these items until the youngsters were out of the nest.

" Intending breeders of Hawfinches should not become unduly worried if nestlings fade out until only one remains. These birds will enthusiastically rear a solitary baby. As a matter of fact, the two youngsters my pairs reared in 1939 were single nestlings.

"Young Hawfinches leave the nest after 12 to 13 days, and when roughly three weeks old they are able to fend for themselves. I made certain they were eating seed and mealworms before separating the youngsters."

When at liberty the Hawfinch feeds upon seeds of all kinds, berries of the yew, hawthorn and others, nuts and beech masts, and insects of various kinds, particularly a smooth caterpillar found among the trees.

Sunflower Seed Much Liked

We must vary the diet of our aviary Hawfinches as much as possible. Their principal food will be sunflower seed, of which they never seem to tire. It should be of the best quality, plump and firm with a good kernal inside.

Offer also canary, hemp, rape, groats, dari, buckwheat and small maize, various nuts, berries from the hedgerow and garden, green peas in the pod, ripe apple and pear, a little watetrcress, chickweed and shepherd's purse.

For soft food give a good brand of insectile mixture. Get them if possible to take this pretty freely as it will be very helpful when the young appear. They must then have mealworms, grubs, caterpillars, small worms and live ants' eggs, and a little sunflower seed and hemp just sprouting.

The hen Hawfinch may be as large as the cock bird but she is not so rich in colour; the crown of the head is ashy brown, with chocolate colour at the back, while as a rule the black bib at the throat is scarcely so large as that of the cock.

Should you be successful in rearing some aviary-bred Hawfinches you must keep your eyes open for any youngsters which look like making up into show birds. An exhibition specimen needs to be well above the average for size, this extra good size being accompanied by richness of colour.

Plumage as Bright as Possible

From the base of the upper mandible to the base of the neck the feathering should be bright chestnut, the cheeks being of the same hue. The back is a rich dark brown and the breast a pale brown with a slight rufous tinge in it. There must be no suggestion of muddiness in breast colouring.

The primary wing feathers in a first-rate specimen are a rich blue-black. When a bird is in high fettle these will carry a lovely gloss. The wing-bar should be well defined, the bib large and well shaped.

The huge mandibles of the Hawfinch vary in colour according to the season of the year, but whatever the colour it will not affect the chances of a really good example staged in grand order.

CHAPTER XII

THE YELLOW BUNTING

THE Yellow Bunting or Yellowhammer has always been a favourite with bird lovers both as a pet and for exhibition purposes. Young Buntings get tame and familiar readily, and for that reason would be best for breeding purposes.

I have found that old birds, even when fairly steady in a cage, tend to become nervous if turned into an aviary or large flight.

The Yellow Bunting is a common bird of the countryside, easily recognised, and familiar along every rural lane and hedgerow. It can be found in cultivated fields and stubbles, where in the winter is consorts with the Sparrows, Greenfinches and others, visiting the farmyards in very severe weather.

What They Feed On

Its food is grain and seeds of all kinds and in the summer, when rearing the young, insects and caterpillars are added to the bill of fare. Very probably the young are fed chiefly upon live food during the first few days of their existence.

The nest of the Yellow Bunting is usually built on or near the ground. It is a rather bulky construction, but beautifully finished and rounded internally. The nests differ a good deal in the material used externally, all those that I have seen (and they are many) having been most neatly lined inside with fine roots and hair.

When put up for breeding in an aviary or flight it would be best to give them a rough gorse branch with coarse grass or heather twisted among it and the whole fastened into a corner, or placed upon the ground.

Let them have fine roots, coarse grass that has been pulled up by the roots and allowed to dry, moss, short lengths of dry grass, and hair.

Although the Yellow Bunting will live for a long time on Canary seed only, it is as well to encourage it to take other seeds so as to give some variety to its diet. One can offer a little rape, lightly-cracked hemp, coarse groats, maw and some wild seed mixture.

It is necessary to give Buntings some live food

Male Yellow Bunting

occasionally, and it will have to be supplied freely when the young are first hatched. For this purpose we require mealworms, gentles, flies, small beetles and grubs generally.

One of the best foods we can give these birds is live ants' cocoons, but, of course, it is not every bird-keeper who can procure them. The next best thing is some dried ones of good quality. Soak them in a little new milk, drain them on a cloth, and give in a small dish on the top of a little good insectile food.

These birds are not particularly keen on green food, although they will nibble a little occasionally and will pick over a bunch of wild food and seeding grass.

The hen Yellow Bunting is not so rich in colour as the cock. She is more greyish green and has only a tinge of yellow on the head and cheeks. Generally she is the more spotted.

Good Markings Important

The type of male bird one should seek for exhibition purposes must be a large specimen with regular and distinct spangling on the back. The excellence of these markings is quite as important as the brightness of the yellow plumage on head and neck.

All Buntings improve considerably with age, not only in size and colour but also in beauty of spangling. For this reason any fancier who succeeds in rearing some of these birds should not part with youngsters for a season or two.

I have found that in the absence of mealworms and other live food, a Yellow Bunting which is being prepared for show will benefit from very small quantities of scraped, raw, lean meat.

F

CHAPTER XIII

THE CORN BUNTING

THE Corn Bunting is the largest of the family, and is fairly common in all open cultivated districts. It is a big, handsome bird, but not a general favourite as a household pet.

Corn Bunting with good markings

As a fancier's bird it occupies a prominent position and good specimens of both sexes are seldom out of the money prizes at the shows. Frequently they have taken the special prize as the best bird in the British section.

No doubt some bird lover will try to breed from a pair; if so they should be fairly steady and must have a small aviary or flight to themselves. They are inclined to be quarrelsome and could not be kept with other birds during the breeding season.

The Corn Bunting nests on the ground, generally among tall grass or corn or under the shelter of a bush on a bank. I would advise a small bundle of twigs, with coarse grass and herbage mixed with it, pushed into a corner of the aviary or flight. The rougher and more natural this could be made to appear, the better. As nesting material offer dry grass, fine roots, " twitch " grass pulled up by the roots, moss and a little hair.

Canary Seed Indispensable

In a state of freedom Corn Buntings undoubtedly feed upon a variety of seeds and insects, but when caged the only seed that appeals to them and of which they never tire is canary, which is probably the nearest approach to grass seed. Of course, there is much more in it, and possibly it is rather more tasty. Anyway, whatever the attraction, it is the one and only seed worth having as far as a Corn Bunting is concerned.

Although canary must be their stock seed it is as well to offer others, but only in small quantities to pick over and select what they fancy. Give small oats, rape, charlock, wild seed mixture, cracked hemp, maw and linseed.

They will eat mealworms, flies, gentles, small beetles and grubs generally. Live ants' cocoons are greatly appreciated, but failing these procure some best quality dry ones and soak them in fresh milk, as advised for the Yellow Bunting.

When they take these pretty freely, it is only another step to get them to eat a good brand of insectile mixture which should in due course be the stock food for rearing purposes.

Sexes Much Alike

There is very little difference in the sexes, the hen usually being somewhat smaller, less bold in head, and more effeminate looking generally. It is thought that they pair for life, so it is as well not to part a likely looking couple even if they fail the first season.

Size, colour and markings are the features to study when selecting a Corn Bunting for exhibition. The arrow-shaped markings should be quite distinct, fairly regular, and plentifully distributed.

Steadiness in this particular species is of the utmost importance, therefore your potential exhibit must be thoroughly well trained. An unsteady specimen runs the risk of being passed by a judge without further consideration.

It quite often happens that Corn Buntings are exhibited in cages which would be none too large for a Yellow Bunting. This is a great mistake. A bird like the Corn requires a reasonably large cage if it is to show itself to the best advantage. It is the smallness of a show cage that often causes these birds to appear clumsy.

CHAPTER XIV

THE CIRL BUNTING

THE Cirl Bunting is one of the most attractive of the Bunting family. It is not so generally distributed as the others, being more a bird of the southern counties, and probably not quite so hardy.

The cock is a very handsome fellow. He has a chestnut breast and a yellow abdomen. His head is olive green, his throat black, his back rich chestnut streaked with black.

The hen is without the black and yellow markings on the face, the throat and breast are striped, and the lesser wing coverts are greenish grey, which is different from the colour of the back.

Shy, but a Potential Breeder

The Cirl Bunting is a somewhat shy bird, and yet it has been bred in captivity. To encourage a pair to nest a small aviary should be allocated, and it should be placed in as sheltered a position as possible.

In a wild state this species builds close to the ground in a thicket of briars and bramble or a gorse bush, or maybe in a hedge bank among the coarse herbage and roots. We can supply the gorse bush and the rough stuff in the aviary, and give them fine roots, dry grass, leaves, coarse grass with roots, and a little moss and hair.

Like all the other Buntings the Cirl is quite content

73

with a generous supply of sound canary seed, but other seeds in small quantities should be offered, and one should be rather liberal with mealworms and other insects.

Insectile food with an extra allowance of sound ants' cocoons mixed with it should be offered pretty freely, as it will lessen the need for quite so much live food. It will be upon these two foods that the successful rearing of the young will mainly depend.

Should the young leave the nest during a cold spell it would be as well to catch them up and keep them comfortable for a time, as they are very susceptible to sudden changes in temperature.

Good Specimen Needed to Win

When exhibited, the Cirl has to compete with all other species of Buntings, therefore unless he is an exceptionally good specimen it is unlikely that he will secure premier honours.

Show points which count most in a Cirl are richness of colouring, clearness of markings, and size above the average. It is very important, of course, that the bird should be well trained so that he remains perfectly steady when under scrutiny by a judge.

CHAPTER XV

THE REED BUNTING

THE only other member of the Bunting family that bird lovers would be likely to try to breed would be the Reed Bunting, a very attractive species and as active and interesting as any of the family.

This bird is usually found near streams and tidal rivers where tall reeds and coarse herbage grow abundantly. But favourite haunts where I have found several nests are disused brick and clay pits.

On the edge of these reeds, long coarse grass, and other vegetation grow quickly, and a pair of these birds will soon take possession when the workmen have gone and the place is quiet.

Untidy Nest Builders

The nest is usually on the ground, or just a few inches above it, in a clump of rushes or strong-growing grass. It is a rather untidy affair and at first glance looks not unlike a heap of rubbish, made as it is of dry grass, withered reeds and rushes, a bit of moss, in fact any flexible, soft vegetation to be found close by. Internally it is finished off with finer grass, hair and usually some dry flowers of the reeds.

A large flight would be quite suitable for a pair of these birds, with a bundle of twigs and rough vegetation such as one could easily collect near a stream or pond.

With these as a foundation and a good supply of material for building, these birds should soon get to work. They pair up early and usually have two nests during a season. They are very devoted to their young and feed well if given the right foodstuffs.

The Reed Bunting should be fed in the same manner as the other Buntings, that is, canary seed as the staple diet, with a little of other seeds as a change, ants' cocoons, insectile food, and live insects, the latter mostly when breeding and rearing young.

The sexes are easily distinguished as the hen lacks the black head and throat and has no yellow tinge on the under part of the body.

The Reed Bunting

CHAPTER XVI

BREEDING SOFTBILLS

THE keeping of softbilled birds in aviaries and cages is not so difficult a matter now as it used to be. In bygone years little was known about the actual requirements of Softbills, especially the migrants. They were simply looked upon as insect eaters, and unsuitable, if not impossible, to keep in cages for any length of time. Now, however, we know that their successful maintenance is simply a matter of suitable accommodation and proper feeding.

The Hardy Species

In looking back, we are apt to wonder how it was that so many of our pet Softbills survived, but on probing into the matter we discover that it was the hardier species which were kept, such as Magpies, Jays, Thrushes, Blackbirds and Larks, birds which when once settled down will thrive upon almost any food within reason.

In the old days the principal foods in use were bread and crushed hemp seed, or bruised rape, raw meat, egg and bread. A particular favourite was a certain concoction termed "German paste," the main ingredients of which were pea meal, dripping, wheat meal and honey, the whole cooked until it was a golden brown. This was given to Blackbirds, Thrushes and

Larks, the latter appearing to thrive on it, possibly because their digestive organs are fairly strong!

Nowadays, however, bird keepers and vendors of foods have used their brains to some purpose, so that we have ready to hand (in normal times) quite a long list of nutritious and eminently suitable foods.

For the larger birds we can use puppy meals and crushed puppy biscuits, best quality chicken meals, and some of the excellent foods put up by well-known firms in packet form ready for immediate use.

For the more delicate migrant Softbills we have the superfine insectile foods which can be purchased at most dealers and bird shops, or obtained direct from the makers.

Although these vary slightly in the ingredients used, most of them contain ants' cocoons, dried flies, silk-worm pupæ, desiccated yolk of egg, with ground biscuit or sponge cake.

Valuable Fresh Fruit

Another great help to successful Softbill keeping is that we can in ordinary times obtain fresh fruit all the year round. Many birds will eat freely of this and thrive upon it, and it is a splendid, natural corrective to the dried ants' cocoons, flies and so forth.

Then occasionally we can make use of grocer's currants and sultanas. These should be first washed in warm water, strained off and gently rubbed in a cloth. They can be added to the staple food or be given separately. Some birds get so fond of them that they waste the staple food hunting for them, so that the latter method is probably better.

Another very nutritious food, and one that is always

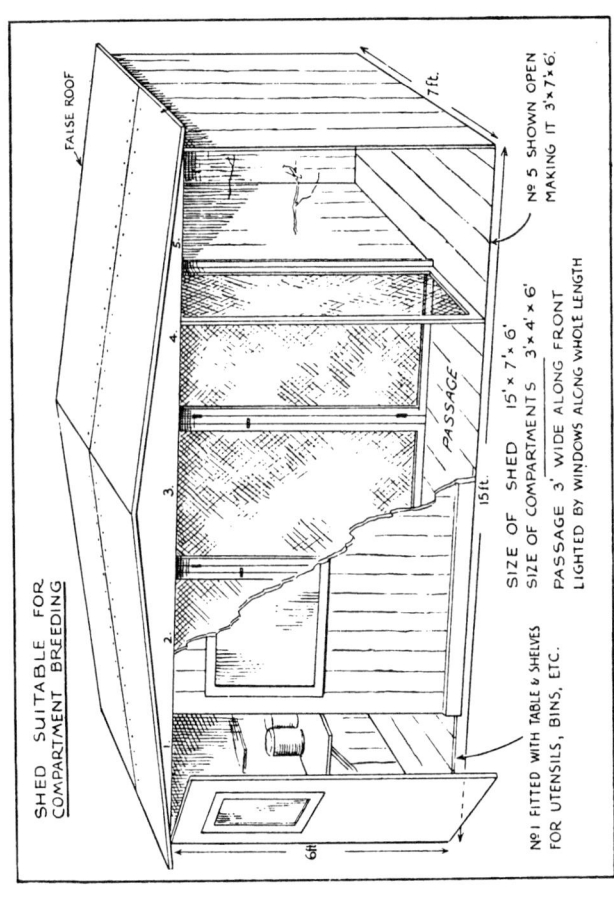

An excellent style of outdoor shed divided up into compartments for Finch breeding

to hand, is cheese. Some good sound Cheddar or Gloster scraped or grated and mixed with the usual food makes a welcome change. Cream cheese can also be made use of; this is, perhaps, better suited to the more delicate species, but the hardier ones will not refuse it.

All Softbills need live food and the more delicate they are the more they need. I have, however, kept some of the commoner and hardier species for months without any, giving instead a tiny morsel of raw, lean meat. If this is quite fresh it will do no harm, used judiciously; it takes the place of the live food and satisfies the bird's natural craving for a change from the usual stock mixture.

How to Get Ants' Cocoons

During the summer months it is possible for bird keepers who live in the country to procure their own fresh ants' cocoons, which are much more valuable as food than the very best of the dried variety, and are just the tit-bit required when young Softbills are hatched.

The ant-hill can be opened and a shovelful of the contents dropped into an airtight box, to be later emptied on the floor of the aviary for the birds to help themselves, taking their fill of insects and cocoons. Alternatively they can be collected and doled out to the birds as required.

A good way to collect them is to choose a sunny day, and lay a sheet of paper on the ground near the anthill. The hill should then be opened with a shovel or small spade and the ants will carry the cocoons to the shelter of the paper, when they can be carefully collected and put in boxes or bags and taken home.

When disturbed the ants are furious and care must be taken not to get them on the hands, or on one's boots and socks. It is advisable to wear an old pair of boots that can be greased or treated with some strong disinfectant. Any surplus ants' cocoons can be dried in a moderate oven and stored for future use.

Wasp grubs form a valuable addition to the birds' diet. They can generally be purchased at a naturalist's store. The hardy and expert fancier may feel inclined to attempt the rather hazardous business of getting them direct from a nest, but it is important to remember that, apart from the personal risk involved, the use of an insecticide may render the grubs poisonous.

Most Birds Like Mealworms

Of all the insects and live food that we can collect, none is quite so useful as the mealworm. This is our staple insect food, procurable at almost any time and not objectionable to handle. All birds will eat mealworms, even Finches, who live mostly on a seed diet.

But mealworms should be given with a certain amount of discretion because the hard, thick skins are rather indigestible. Thus the larger worms should be used for the more robust birds and the smaller ones for the more delicate species.

Bird-keepers who have several Softbills should breed their own mealworms, at least in sufficient quantity to help the supply. Many years ago I used to get mine from an old mill. I was allowed to hunt around in dark corners and odd places, and sometimes made a big find among some old sacks.

Mealworms turn up when least expected. For a time I kept some Softbills in an outhouse, while a proper bird room was being constructed, and some months later I found quite a quantity of worms and beetles in that shed. Some of the mealworms had escaped from the birds and established themselves in a corner, there breeding and multiplying.

To breed them under control is not a difficult matter, but some patience is required. There are several methods, of which the following is as good as any :

Procure a couple of rather flat wooden boxes about two feet square, and make lids to fit with a flange all round them to prevent the mealworms escaping. Cut a hole in the centre about three inches square and cover this with a piece of fine perforated zinc (this is for ventilation). Cut some coarse sacking twice the size of the floor space of the box, so that when folded it fits inside closely but not tightly.

Add Oats, Bran and Meal

Put into the box a layer of crushed oats, bran and meal, about an inch and a half thick, then the folded sacking, and on this a sheet of coarse brown paper. Another layer of the oats and meal follows, more sacking and paper, then more meal, and this should be continued until the box is three parts full. Then turn in a pint or so of mealworms.

Some breeders soak the paper and one or two of the sacks in beer and treacle, allowing it to dry in well before using. The boxes should now be placed in a fairly warm position, such as a cupboard near a fireplace, under the hot-water pipes of a greenhouse, or in some similar location.

They should be left undisturbed for some months as it takes about a year for the worms to change to beetles and the beetles to lay the eggs that hatch and produce the worms again.

Sometimes during the summer months one is able to obtain the beetles, and if so this shortens the period of production considerably. Occasionally, a new box should be started from the contents of the old one, a job best carried out in the winter.

In addition to the live food named, there is a good deal that can be collected by the keen bird-keeper, such as house flies, beetles, caterpillars, earwigs, greenfly, small earth worms and other creatures.

A garden aviary for Softbills with an open flight bridging a small stream at which the birds could drink and bathe. Nesting would take place in the shelter portion, if suitably equipped

CHAPTER XVII

THE MAGPIE, JAY AND JACKDAW

THE two largest of our Softbills that any bird-keeper would be likely to try to breed with are the Magpie and Jay. Both species are well worth keeping. They are not only particularly handsome but very interesting and make most delightful pets. They are splendid mimics, and if kept in a suitable garden enclosure are cheerful and entertaining.

To breed with a pair with any hope of success a fair-sized aviary would have to be given up to them, and the prospective parents should be young birds if possible.

Secretive Nesters

In a wild state they are very secretive and wily in their nesting, and therefore some attempt should be made to enable them to nest in seclusion. A good thick bush of faggots might be placed in one corner of the aviary, and if a board can be fastened up to screen it somewhat, so much the better. The birds will appreciate this quiet corner.

Magpies must be supplied with quite a quantity of sticks of various kinds; some thorn branches should be included as these are the favourites, and most used for the roof or dome of the nest.

These sticks are cemented together with mud and clay, so a lump of clay in a shallow pan of water will be welcomed. When the nest is well on the way supply plenty of fine fibrous roots for the lining.

The only difference in the sexes that I have noticed is the slightly smaller size of the hen bird. Her plumage is not quite so lustrous, especially in the spring and early summer, when the cock looks his best.

A similar bush or bundle of faggots should be included in an enclosure devoted to a pair of Jays, but in their case some evergreens, such as holly or yew, should be included. The nest will be formed externally of twigs and sticks and lined with fibrous roots.

Two young Magpies bred in a London Fancier's aviary

G

Winter scene showing Jays eating acorns

Both Magpies and Jays can be fed upon a good brand of chicken meal, as used to rear young chicks, Pheasant meal or crushed puppy biscuits made crumbly moist with hot water, or a little gravy for a change.

Give scraps from the table such as suet, rice and other puddings, boiled potatoes and vegetables, brown bread and milk, occasionally a very little lean meat, smashed nuts, acorns, wheat, fruit and berries of various kinds, a freshly killed mouse, beetles, caterpillars, mealworms and other live food.

A pair of Jackdaws can be fed in the same way. For breeding they would need an aviary to themselves and a good-sized nest-box with an entrance hole at the side would possibly suit them as well as anything. This could be covered roughly with virgin cork to give it some resemblance to a tree trunk.

The nesting material for these birds will be almost anything that they can carry, but it is as well to supply them with sticks, straw, hay, long grass, clods pulled up by the roots, moss, wool and feathers.

The difference in the sexes is that the hen is rather smaller than the cock and the grey collar is not quite so clear and distinct.

Anything bright has a fascination for a Jackdaw. This bird is investigating the metal fittings of a handbag

CHAPTER XVIII

THE SONG THRUSH

THE most popular bird among Softbills is, undoubtedly, the Song Thrush, a big, bold, handsome fellow whose spotted breast and intelligent eye make him conspicuous among others. He is not only noted for his beauty of form and feather; as a musician he takes high rank.

He is a constant performer, singing in the spring and early summer from daylight till dusk, and he is generally the last of the feathered choir to be heard. Little wonder that he is such a prime favourite and so much in demand as a pet.

Superb Show Bird

As an exhibition bird he is splendid, usually fearless and showing himself to perfection when being judged. But as he needs a fair-sized cage, which is not easily conveyed any distance, we do not see so many of these birds at exhibitions as we should like.

The Song Thrush has bred in captivity and I feel sure that a good many more will be produced in the future. A pair of young birds should be selected and caged some time before they are turned into an aviary or large flight.

A rough bundle of branches with evergreens intermixed should be placed in a suitable position. They would make no fuss about building in this, as in a wild state their nests have been constructed in all sorts of

88

positions. I have found them myself in evergreens,
heaps of rough branches in a faggot stack, against a
wall, just supported by a branch or two of ivy; even on
the ground and at the top of a bank.

If an old nest can be found and pushed into the

Song Thrush feeding young at her nest in a planted aviary

centre of the bundle it would encourage them. The material supplied for nest-making should be plenty of twigs and dry grass, a little moss and dead leaves. When this is worked into shape a lining of mud will be put in, and into this some wet rotten wood.

The mud for lining can be supplied by having a shallow pan of water with a lump of clay in it, and a small decayed branch will give them all the wood they require. In hot, dry summers I have noticed that the mud lining is sometimes omitted; this may be due to a scarcity of mud, or perhaps to the birds' instinct telling them that it is not needed for warmth.

Hens Become Very Tame

The hen is a close sitter and even when at liberty will allow one to pass quite close to the nest. If you pretend not to see her she appears quite content and has no thought of danger while incubating. Should she be used to you, you can do almost anything with the young when they are hatched. I have frequently given nestlings a small worm with the mother Thrush a few feet away looking on approvingly.

The feeding of the Song Thrush is not a very difficult matter; soft food is needed, with fruit and insects. The soft food can consist of a good brand of chicken meal—not the kind given to adult birds, but that used for the rearing of young chicks. This should be made crumbly moist with hot water. By way of variety a little hard-boiled egg or a few ants' cocoons can be added to it.

Another good food is crushed puppy biscuits, and then there are the excellent foods put up in packets by well-known firms. Thus a suitable staple diet is not at all a difficult matter to provide.

Fruit can be offered in season and live food in moderation. If one is too liberal with live food it becomes a necessity to them, and they go soft if the usual quantity is not always on hand.

Hints on Sexing

It is somewhat difficult to sex this species, but one is able to distinguish the cock more by his manner, actions and song than by any special markings.

Ring Ouzels have been successfully bred in one of Mr. P. Carr's aviaries. Here the hen is seen feeding her nestlings

CHAPTER XIX

THE BLACKBIRD

PRESSING the Song Thrush hard for popularity as a pet is the Blackbird, a splendid fellow with his glossy black coat and golden bill. A glorious songster well known to everybody, he sings at his best when his mate is sitting within hearing on her clutch of bluish-green eggs, mottled with reddish-brown.

The Blackbird is not quite such an early nester as the Song Thrush, being more of a late spring bird, and I am doubtful if he is quite so hardy as the Thrush, although quite able, of course, to withstand wintry conditions in an outside enclosure.

Young Birds Preferable

For breeding in an aviary or large flight young birds should be chosen. These can be distinguished by the reddish tinge to the primary wing feathers, which are not dead black until after the second moult. The hen has a brown beak, is not so black generally as the cock, and is mottled on the breast.

There should be no difficulty in getting these birds to nest in a bush of branches and evergreens, as the latter are favourites with them in a wild state. They also go for sites along the hedgerow where rough trimmings have been pushed into a gap for repairs.

In fact, they are not at all particular as to the location of their home; the most unlikely place will often take their fancy, so with a little encouragement they should build in the aviary.

92

Supply the pair with plenty of dry grass, a few twigs and moss, and the nest they build will be plastered inside with mud and then lined with more dry grass.

The stock food advised for the Thrush suits the Blackbird quite well, but one should occasionally add

The shapely and tuneful Blackbird

a portion of insectile food to it, giving also a little more live food, especially when getting them into breeding condition.

The Blackbird eats more fruit than the Thrush and should have his share of anything that is in season, such as sweet cherries, currants, strawberries, raspberries, apples and pears, both of the latter given a bit over-ripe.

It will be advisable to improve the stock food a little when the young first arrive. This can be done by the addition of a little insectile food or hard-boiled yolk of egg well mixed into the food with a fork.

CHAPTER XX

THE STARLING

STARLINGS pair for life, so any bird lover who intends to breed with a pair should begin with young birds, keeping them together while they are in good health.

When in full breeding plumage the Starling is a handsome fellow

These birds like to nest under cover; they select holes in trees, walls and old buildings. A colony of them will take possession of a barn roof or church steeple, and rear numbers of young ones. They are very prolific and will continue to lay clutch after clutch until the autumn moult puts them out of action.

A pair should do well in a big flight. A wooden box for nesting should be about 18 inches square with a hole in one side for entrance; or one side could simply be left open and have a piece of board nailed across at the bottom to keep the nesting material in place. This arrangement would allow more light to the interior, and would facilitate cleaning it out when necessary.

Leave Nest Boxes in Flight

The nesting box should be left in the flight all the year round as the old birds frequently visit the nesting site and roost in it, and they will be ready to start again early the next season.

One need not be particular about the building materials supplied; straw, grass and fine roots would perhaps be the best, with a few feathers for lining.

The hen Starling is, as a rule, rather heavier in build than the cock, and is more profusely spotted; these spots are somewhat larger, which gives her a lighter appearance. The cock bird is smarter, rather richer in colour, and has more sheen on his plumage.

The young birds, until the moult, are quite unlike the parents, being a brownish-grey colour all over except on the breast and underparts, which are white.

CHAPTER XXI

THE SMALLER SOFTBILLS

BIRD-KEEPERS need not confine their breeding of Softbills to the larger species only. Several of the smaller and equally beautiful birds have at various times been bred under controlled conditions.

The smaller examples are, if anything, more valuable as cage birds, both as singing pets and for exhibition purposes. In the bird room they can be kept in smaller flights and cages and are much more easily conveyed to and from the shows.

All Likely Nesters

Among a few of the species that have been bred are Larks, Pipits, Spotted Flycatchers, Hedge Sparrows and Bearded Reedlings. If these can be successfully reared there is no reason why several others should not. In the case of Skylarks these have been bred in an ordinary cage of reasonable length, when they made their nest in a hollowed turf.

A long flight would be quite suitable for a pair, with a turf at one end hollowed in the middle, this cavity being surrounded by a handful or two of coarse herbage to give a little shelter.

Skylarks are not difficult birds to breed. The same soft food as given to the larger species will meet their needs, with a spoonful of insectile food in it when getting them into condition, or when they are feeding young. A little chopped hard-boiled egg could be added for a change.

They will eat various seeds and green food and should have a mealworm or two, live ants' cocoons, grubs and earwigs. The cock is usually a larger, bolder, more upstanding bird than the hen, with longer wings.

Another glorious songster is the Woodlark, and a pair of these might be treated in much the same manner as the Skylark. But I have found them to be rather

Spotted Flycatcher at its nest in a wall cavity

more delicate feeders and to require a somewhat better stock mixture.

They usually nest on the ground, but not in such open situations as the Skylark; in a flight, however, the same arrangements for nesting should be suitable. Dried grass, moss and cow hair are the materials used in constructing the nest.

Woodlark at its nest containing three babies

The Hedge Sparrow, in my opinion, has been very much neglected as a cage bird. The cock is not to be despised as a songster, for although he has little variety in his song, it is sweet and soft and has a joyous ring.

As an exhibition bird he has, unfortunately, had to compete with rarer and more attractively coloured Soft-bills for premier honours, but I see no reason why in the future these birds should not have a class to themselves at some of the larger shows.

The cock in full plumage is a decidedly attractive bird, and as the species would breed freely in flights, from an exhibition standpoint these birds would soon be very much improved by careful selection of stock. They are very hardy, and may be kept under almost any conditions.

Hedge Sparrows nest early in the year, usually before there are any leaves on the hedgerows and bushes, and so one frequently finds a nesting site in a heap of hedge trimmings or branches. Thus it should take readily to a small bundle of evergreens and branches in a flight.

The birds will need to be supplied with fine roots, dead grass, moss, and wool, hair and feathers for the nest lining. The finished article is a charming little affair, and when filled with its clutch of clear blue eggs possesses a beauty all its own.

Diet Presents no Difficulty

Another reason why the Hedge Sparrow should be a popular breeding species is the ease with which it can be fed. It should have a good brand of chick meal made moist, various seeds including a wild mixture, and a mealworm or two occasionally.

In the breeding season the soft food could be varied by the addition of a little meat meal, chopped suet or hard-boiled egg. Fruit, berries and seeding wild plants should be offered. During the winter months it will do quite well on the soft food and seeds.

Among the rarer Softbills Bearded Reedlings have been reared in a good-sized aviary, the parents being fed upon insectile food with an extra allowance of ants' cocoons and occasionally a little hard-boiled yolk of egg. Various seeds, including maw, were also given.

CHAPTER XXII

HINTS ON HAND-REARING

THERE may be times when parent birds refuse to feed the young, or carry out their duties in such a half-hearted manner that a fancier decides to rear the nestlings himself.

Young Finches can be reared by good feeding hen Canaries, and the babies need not always have been hatched out by their foster-parents.

For instance, a nest of young Goldfinches about three days old was once found in an apple tree. The chicks were taken home and given to a pair of Canaries, whose own eggs were removed. The whole brood was successfully reared on the same food as given to rear young Canaries.

Best Time to Commence

Young British birds can be reared at any age. I have reared them myself from three days old and also finished them off from a fortnight to three weeks. But given the choice of the time to start rearing it should be just as the eyes begin to open.

The nest with the brood in it should be put into a shallow box and covered with flannel for warmth, unless it is thought to be advisable to leave the nest for the parent birds to start raising another family.

In this case a nest should be made in the box, an ordinary lined nest-pan being used with a little moss and hair. If these materials are worked round with the hand quite a good nest can be formed.

The soft foods for rearing will vary somewhat according to the species, but personally I prefer hard-boiled egg and biscuits for this job. The egg should be boiled for ten minutes. When cold, well mix with a fork the yolk and part of the white into two crushed biscuits, and to this add a dessert-spoonful of best ants' cocoons, free from rubbish.

Three young hand-reared Thrushes gaping for food

There are several other foods, normally intended for the rearing of Canaries, that can be used, but I find that not all of them are quite so satisfactory to handle, since they are apt to fall off the feeding stick while being used.

A feeding stick, by the way, can be made out of a

II

flat stick, shaping it with a knife to about three-sixteenths of an inch at one end, and, of course, flat so that the food will stay on. The point should be rounded.

Take a little of the mixture and make the food fairly wet with fresh milk. Get a scrap on the stick, and when the birds gape for food (which they will do directly you touch them) put the mixture well into the mouth, but be careful not to injure the sensitive lining or the tongue.

Frequent Meals Needed

Feed a little at a time, and often, according to the age of the birds; the younger they are the more frequently they must be fed. Once every hour is a general rule, gradually increasing the time to every two hours as they grow.

The very first feed in the morning should be a small one, after which the nestlings appear to wake up and will then take a larger quantity. During the day they do not need much, but about four o'clock in the after-

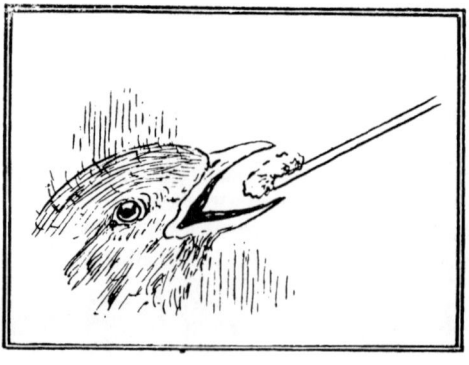

A Feeding Stick

There is no difficulty in shaping a small piece of wood to serve as a feeding stick

noon you can begin to pack them with food for the night so that they go to sleep with full crops.

It is important that the brood be kept warm and clean. If it is a large one they naturally make each other warm, but if there are only one or two, they should be well covered up with a layer of flannel and put near a hot-water pipe, or bottle, at night.

As soon as they begin to sit on the edge of the nest or get out of it, they should be removed to a cage, the nest placed in one corner, and some soft food put on the floor of the cage.

When mealtime comes, try to feed them from the pan of food and encourage them to peck at it. As soon as one starts feeding, the others will quickly follow.

Continue with Soft Food

When they can feed themselves, continue to give them soft food until they can crack seed, and even then offer them a little occasionally, letting them have it in a fairly dry state.

When hand-rearing Softbills, in addition to the soft food, a few ants' cocoons should be dropped into the mouth with small pair of tweezers, and they can also be given tiny mealworms or parts of the larger ones dipped in milk.

CHAPTER XXIII

RINGING YOUNG BIRDS

FOR many years now it has been the custom for breeders of Canaries, Hybrids and British birds to mark their young stock by means of rings placed on the leg for identification purposes. These rings are made to clip round the shank of the bird just as it leaves the nest, and can easily be removed at any time if it becomes necessary.

In some Societies closed rings are placed on birds intended for competition, for certain cups and trophies. These rings must be put on the birds while they are still in the nest, and if removed afterwards they cannot be refitted.

What the Law Demands

Under the provisions of the Protection of Birds Act, 1933, it is necessary to fit a closed ring on the leg of all cage- and aviary-bred British birds intended for sale, though not for exhibition if there is no intention to sell them.

The best plan, then, is to ring *all* young birds bred in captivity, as no fancier can tell for certain if a bird is going to develop into a champion or not.

The rings used for most of the Finches will be of the same size as are now in use for Canaries and Hybrids. The Hawfinch, Buntings, Larks, Blackbirds and Thrushes would naturally need rings somewhat larger. It is impossible to give the exact age for putting on the rings, but usually it is from six to nine days.

A Greenfinch, for instance, with its larger feet would

need to be rung a day or so earlier than a Goldfinch or Redpoll. There is a risk of the ring slipping off if put on too soon, and if left too late it is somewhat difficult to get on.

When ringing is left rather late the ring may be warmed in hot water, when the slight expansion caused will help to make fitting easy. The rings should be laid out all ready, so that there is no fuss or flurry over the operation.

Take the baby bird in the left hand so that you have the leg and foot quite free; slip the ring carefully over the three front claws, then over the ball of the foot, and up the shank, taking the hind claw with it. When it is past the hind claw, the latter can be released and the job is completed.

When to Fit Rings

The best time to carry out ringing is in the evening, as the old bird will settle down on the young when they are returned without being too inquisitive. It is a good plan to have a nice big bunch of seeding wild food to offer the birds, not only to entice the hens off their nests but also to keep them busy while you are ringing the nestlings.

This ringing business used to be rather a delicate operation requiring great care, but latterly a new method of fitting these leg circlets has been discovered and the British bird fancier should endeavour to witness a demonstration of this latest process.

I hope that some day a clever ring-maker will put on the market a ring which can be fitted as the birds leave the nest—one that will lock itself and not be removable except by filing.

Standards and Scales of Points for Exhibition British Birds

THE BLACKBIRD

Size :	.. ..	15
Shape :	Wide, rounded chest, good width of skull ..	20
Colour :	A deep rich black, not dull or rusty	20
Beak & Eye :	The beak a good clear golden colour, eye bold, with prominent cere	10
Condition :	.. ..	20
Steadiness :	.. ..	15

THE BLACKCAP

Size :	.. ..	10
Shape :	Chubby, but graceful	10
Cap :	To be clean cut and as black as possible	10
Condition :	Feather close and compact : the wing and tail perfect : no frayed or broken plumage ..	50
Steadiness :	.. ..	20

BULLFINCH

Size :	.. ..	10
Shape :	As thick and chubby as possible, with short, thick neck	15
Head :	Broad, with clean-cut cap	10
Back & Wings :	Back colour bright and clear, free from smoky appearance : wings carried close, with the bars well defined	15
Body :	Breast colour to be as rich and bright as possible ..	25
Condition :	Feather to be soft and silky the colours throughout to be deep and glossy	15
Steadiness :	.. ..	10

THE CHAFFINCH

Size :	.. ..	10
Shape :	Fairly stout	10
Head & Body :	The cap to be bright, and as blue as possible : back warm and rich : breast colour to be rich and bright	20
Wings :	The markings to be clean cut and showing the yellow in flights and white on shoulder conspicuously	10
Condition :	.. ..	20
Steadiness :	.. ..	30

CORN BUNTING

Size :	.. ..	5
Shape :	Large, very chubby body and bold head	5
Markings :	Bold and distinct : the arrows on the breast of good shape and regular	20
Colour :	.. ..	10
Condition :	.. ..	10
Steadiness :	.. ..	50

THE GOLDFINCH

Size :	.. ..	5
Shape :	Well proportioned : not too stout or angular nor thick at waist : to stand at an angle of 45 deg. on perch	20
Head & Blaze :	Head fairly large, with wide skull : blaze large, well back over eye and down the throat, free from black stripes or breaks and as rich as possible in colour	20
Wings :	Bars large and bright : buttons well defined and regular	15
Body :	Colours to be as clear and pure and well-contrasted as possible, especially on breast, where the marking should be even : other markings clean cut and pure in colour	10
Condition :	Healthy : tight in feather, no broken or missing plumage	20
Steadiness :	.. ..	10

THE GREENFINCH

Size :	.. ..	10
Shape :	To be shapely and well proportioned, and stand fairly erect	20
Wings :	To be carried close, with rich yellow bars and black markings distinct .. .. :	10
Colour :	The yellow to be bright and plentiful ; the green and grey-green on body, wings and head to be clear and bright as possible	20
Condition :	Feathers tight and clean, showing plenty of quality	20
Steadiness :	.. ..	20

THE HAWFINCH

Size :	.. ..	10
Head :	To be large and broad with bold eye, and evenly coloured all over : the black between beak and eye to be deep and clean cut : the bib to be triangular in shape and clear at edges	25
Wings :	To be carried close, with the bars well defined ..	10
Condition & Colour :	As tight as possible in feather : the colours throughout to be clean and bright	25
Steadiness :	.. ..	30

THE LINNET

Size :	.. ..	10
Shape & Position :	To be well proportioned : to stand well up from the perch	10
Markings :	To be clear and well defined, especially on breast, small in the centre and larger at the sides, extending well down the thighs	20
Wings, etc. :	To be carried close, and be spangled at the tips, the white to show distinctly, also in the tail, and the latter should be close and compact	10
Colour :	A rich brown, to be well distributed	15
Condition :	.. ..	15
Steadiness :	.. ..	20

THE NIGHTINGALE

Size :	.. ..	20
Shape :	Somewhat stout and bold	15
Colour :	The red on the rump as bright as possible : other colours pure	15
Condition :	.. ..	30
Steadiness :	.. ..	20

REED BUNTING

Size :	.. ..	10
Shape :	Bold head, good width of chest	10
Markings :	The bib to be clean-cut and as black as possible : the markings on back and wings distinct	20
Colour :	The white as pure as possible and the brown on the back rich, and well distributed	10
Condition :	.. ..	10
Steadiness :	.. ..	40

THE REDPOLL

Size :	.. ..	20
Shape :	Fairly stout, and to stand as erect as possible ..	15
Markings :	All the markings to be clear and well defined : those on the breast to be as plentiful as possible : the wings to be well carried, showing a distinct bar	30
Condition & Colour :	Deep and rich as possible	25
Steadiness :	.. ..	10

THE SISKIN

Size :	.. ..	10
Shape :	To be fairly stout, and not crouch on the perch ..	10
Head :	The cap to be jet black, showing faint, even lacing, and clean cut : the bib as distinct as possible ..	15
Wings & Tail :	To show plenty of yellow bars, the black feathers deep in colour and all markings clear	15
Body Markings :	Plentiful and regular, extending well down the thighs	10
Colour :	The yellow on head and breast to be as clear and bright as possible, free from smoky appearance ..	20
Condition :	.. ..	10
Steadiness :	.. ..	10

THE STARLING

Size :	.. ..	15
Shape :	.. ..	15
Markings :	The spangling to be regular and clear, and just large enough to show distinctly against the ground colour	30
Colour & Condition :	Feathers close and compact showing a rich gloss ..	25
Steadiness :	.. ..	15

I

THE THRUSH

Size :	.. ..	10
Shape & *Carriage :*	Very thick-set and well-rounded in build, nice jaunty movement	20
Markings :	The markings round the head and throat should be as distinct as possible : on the breast clear and bold and running from throat to vent, or nearly so : the wings close and well carried	30
Colour :	.. ..	5
Condition :	Feathers close and compact, not broken or frayed ..	20
Steadiness :	.. ..	15

THE TWITE

Size :	.. ..	15
Shape :	.. ..	10
Markings :	To be bold and distinct : the breast well covered and regular	30
Condition & *Colour :*	.. ..	20
Steadiness :	.. ..	25

YELLOW BUNTING

Size :	.. ..	10
Shape :	Rather stout, of easy carriage	10
Markings :	The V-shaped stripes above the eyes to show clearly : the cheek markings and the markings on back and wings to be well defined : the spots on the shoulder and markings on back and wings to be regular and bold	20
Colour :	The yellow to be pure and rich : the brown as bright as possible	20
Condition :	.. ..	10
Steadiness :	.. ..	30

In mid-Victorian days our grandparents fed their Canaries, Parrots, and other feathered pets on "Hyde's Bird Seeds." To-day, as in the 70's, Hyde's is still unsurpassed for maintaining Canaries, Budgerigars and other cage birds in health and fine condition.

Hyde's BIRD SEEDS

Sold in 1/- and 2/- cartons by all dealers

R. HYDE & CO. LTD.

61 LILFORD ROAD, LONDON, S.E.5

ALL BIRDS NEED HELP

in the matter of eliminating waste body matter. Unless this is eliminated, toxic poisoning is set up with usually fatal results. Birds in captivity have to exist largely on dried seeds and starchy foods, a diet very different from their natural one. They too usually have far less exercise than they get in the wild state.

POWDER DWEK eliminates body poisons in a safe and easy way. It contains two miracle working compounds. One liberates a powerful yet harmless germicide and destroys all bacteria. The other forms a soothing protective coating over the whole of the intestinal tract, allaying inflammation, neutralising toxins and waste food matter. **Powder Dwek is 2/11, 5/5, 10/3½** 16/8 (half pound), 31/3 (pound), **Liquid Dwek 3/2, 6/-, 9/9**

Birds need minerals too. **EXONIA** is a tonic mineral food containing 7 elements which all birds need to keep them fighting fit. **Exonia is 2/5, 4/5½, 7/11, 15/3 a bottle.**

CALCI is another mineral food supplement. This ensures birds get the minerals they would normally get in the wild. **Calci is** 2/7 per pound.

Prices are post paid. When writing enclose an extra 1d. for my new pamphlet " THE WAY TO BIRD HEALTH." The advice in it is worth pounds

PERCY GLOVER, F.Z.S., Broadlands, Fareham, Hants

INSTRUCTIVE BOOKS ON BIRDKEEPING

	Price	By Post
"The Budgerigar in Captivity" (Ninth Edition)	2/6	2/9
"Budgerigars and How to Breed Them"	2/-	2/3
"Colour Breeding in Budgerigars"	6d.	8d.
"The Budgerigar Breeding and Show Register"	1/-	1/2
"Talking Budgerigars and How to Train Them"... ...	6d.	8d.
Budgerigar Breeders' Pedigree Forms (1 doz. per book)...	6d.	8d.
"Canary Breeding for Beginners (14th Edition)	2/6	2/9
"The Border Fancy Canary"	2/6	2/9
"The Roller Canary" by Gutierrez	2/-	2/2
"Canary Breeding Room Register"	1/-	1/2
"Foreign Birds for Beginners" (Seventh Edition)	1/6	1/8
"Aviaries, Bird-Rooms and Cages"	2/6	2/10
"Bird Ailments and Accidents"	1/6	1/9

Obtainable through all Newsagents or direct from the Publishers

COLOURED PLATES

Sets of Coloured Plates of Canaries, Budgerigars, Foreign, British,
Mules and Hybrids and Aquaria, available from the Publishers.
───────Send for detailed catalogue.───────

CAGE BIRDS, DORSET HOUSE, STAMFORD ST., LONDON, S.E.1

Printed in the United Kingdom
by Lightning Source UK Ltd.
135906UK00001B/178/A